IT'S ONLY NATURAL

F. M. Drew

© Copyright 2003 F. M. Drew
The right of F. M. Drew to be identified as the author of this work has been asserted in accordance with the Copyright, Designs and Patents Act 1988.

All rights reserved. No reproduction, copy or transmission of this publication may be made without written permission. No paragraph of this publication may be reproduced, copied or transmitted save with the written permission or in accordance with the provisions of the Copyright Act 1956 (as amended). Any person who does any unauthorised act in relation to this publication may be liable to criminal prosecution and civil claims for damage.

First Century 405 Kings Road London SW10 0BB
and
27 Greenhead Road Huddersfield West Yorkshire HD1 4EN
an imprint of First Century Ltd.

Website: www.first-century.co.uk

E mail: Info@first-cntury.co.uk

ISBN 1-903930-46-4

DEDICATION

This book is dedicated firstly to my husband who has had to endure twenty years of going through this search with me. He has had to put up with my many moments of frustration and anger and has, somehow managed to keep his sanity. Thank you, Ben, for always listening.

Secondly I dedicate this book to the two people who brought me up. Namely my adopted parents, or to use their deserved titles, my mother and my late father. Thank you both for having me.

CONTENTS

Mary Brown		5
Introduction		9
Chapter 1	Sparks	16
Chapter 2:	The Journey Begins	27
Chapter 3:	The Breakthrough	34
Chapter 4:	The First Reunion	47
Chapter 5:	Success	55
Chapter 6:	Roland	67
Chapter 7:	Home Truths	75
Chapter 8:	Secrets and Spies	88
Chapter 9:	Births and Deaths	101
Chapter 10:	Found and Lost	112
Chapter 11:	Behind Closed Doors	124
Chapter 12:	Boundaries	137
Chapter 13:	Full Circle	146
Useful Addresses		155

MARY BROWN (London 1960s)

The procedure was always the same. First she would hear rustling and movement; that would be the social worker preparing the room for clients. Mary imagined her fluffing up cushions on a comfortable, homely settee and arranging magazines on a coffee table. Shortly, the smell of fresh coffee would creep under the door and fill the little room in which she waited.

A soft murmur of voices, all a little too quiet to make out any words clearly, broken only by intermittent laughter. Gentle, happy laughter that came from the hidden world that existed on the other side of the door. Mary liked to think of "Cubicle 7" as her "purgatory." Beyond was the world in which she wanted to live but one that always eluded her.

The moment she smelled the coffee, it would be time. Ten minutes and it would all be over. There was no smell of coffee as yet; instead she had noticed that "Cubicle 7" had a peculiar aroma of its own. A mixture of stale tobacco and soiled nappies. A dirty smell for a dirty people, she thought. The scent of shame, she thought. For Mary Brown knew she was not a "good girl". Good girls never visited a place like this. The odour that filled her nostrils came only from desperate, frightened women who shared the same secret.

Except for one wooden stool, "Cubicle 7" at the Kingston Social Services was bare. Mary Brown sat on that stool, cradling a tiny infant in her arms and staring blankly at a blistered and peeling magnolia painted wall ahead of her.

In her thirties, she wore a beige mackintosh over a plain blue blouse and brown checked shirt. Normally she would not wear such conservative clothes, a mini skirt and knee high boots were more her style and showed off her shapely legs. Today, however, she did not wish to show any part of her body to anyone. To remain unnoticed was of paramount importance.

Mary closed her eyes and listened carefully. Not a sound. The total silence seemed only to magnify thoughts of hopelessness, which filled her head and tormented her. A drink might quieten her nerves. She reached down inside her mackintosh pocket and took out a tiny perfume bottle marked "Eau de toilette". Mary drank the contents of the bottle and quickly placed the bottle back in her pocket. The tiny quantity of gin that she had managed to pour in to the bottle that morning was not enough to numb her; anxiety still rose up within her.

The baby seemed to feel her tension and began whimpering. Mary did not glance at the infant. It could wait. She knew it would not be long before the child had a feed, a good feed. This baby would not go hungry again.

The smell of coffee sweetened the air around her. Its welcoming aroma masked the despair that filled her mind. It would be soon now.

She glanced at the baby. As on previous occasions she had dressed the infant well. Spending the little money she could find to purchase new, pure white baby clothes.

Cradling the child in one arm, she reached awkwardly into another pocket and pulled out a comb. Wanting to make a good impression she tied back a mass of dark curls that had fallen over her forehead.

"Are you ready?" A voice broke the silence. It was Mary's social worker who entered the cubicle from a main corridor. She wheeled in a trolley with a changing mat, a blanket and some nappies.

"It's time, Mary." Mary nodded and stood. Holding the baby close to her now she leaned forward and gently kissed the child on the lips.

The social worker did not rush her. She knew that Mary might not stay calm. She knew Mary well, even had a certain fondness for her. It was not often, seldom ever, that a social worker had the chance to work with this type of client case over and over again.

"I have brought a few of baby's things," Mary said thrusting a small paper parcel into the woman's hand. "It's nothing really, just a toy and a picture." She did not answer. Mary always did this even though she knew the rules. It was best just to accept them.

"It's time for you to go now."

Mary felt tears welling up in her large blue eyes. They gathered speed and rolled down her face, dropping on to the baby's head. Whether it was the tears or the fact that she now held the baby so tightly against her, Mary was not sure but, as if on cue, the infant began to howl. This seemed a fitting time to hand over her baby.

Mary did not say goodbye; she could not think of words that sounded sensible and so leaving the door ajar simply walked away. The sound of her baby crying caused her breasts to leak milk and the tears pooling in her eyes blurred her vision to the point where she was unable to see the people who stared at her as she made her way to the exit.

The social worker closed the door to "Cubicle 7" and lay the baby down on the changing trolley. Carefully she removed the baby's clothing and collecting a bin liner hidden underneath the trolley, placed all the infant's clothes in it. She unwrapped the little parcel Mary had given her to find a soft brown teddy and a picture. The picture was of Mary; it showed her to be a tall, elegant woman with large smiley blue eyes and a mass of curly black hair. In her arms she held a kitten. The social worker knew the rules only too well and, before allowing herself to even question them, placed the toy and the picture into the bin bag with the baby's clothes.

Having checked the infant over she then wrapped the child in a soft yellow blanket. Collecting some keys from her pocket she unlocked an adjoining door. As she opened it, sunlight poured in. The room that lay beyond had many windows and was colourful and welcoming. It had a clock and pictures of children all over the walls. It also had the sofa that Mary imagined and on the recently fluffed up cushions sat the social worker's other clients.

She lifted the baby up into her arms and walked through to join them. As she appeared a man and woman stood up to greet her. The social worker smiled reassuringly at the couple and then handed the infant over to them.

As human beings, we grow up and make our own families. The moment a new baby is born there is a flurry of suggestions as to who that baby takes after. Whether he has his father's or mother's eyes, his uncle's nose, his grandfather's ears or his auntie's sense of humour. All debatable and all fascinating to the immediate family. The need to belong, to be part of a structure of a family, with its own unique history in time, is within us all.

It is the essence of a family. Each set of genes re-born into the next generation, present slightly different characteristics and personality traits, but all can be recognised and are familiar to that particular family.

Unless, of course you are adopted!

INTRODUCTION

Just forty years ago the idea that women could be accepted in society as single parents would have seemed impossible. Emphasis was placed firmly on marriage and children being born within that union. To be an unmarried pregnant woman was a scandal. Abortion although available on the "back street" was not accepted in the way it is today and the contraceptive pill was a new concept. The sexual revolution was about to happen, but up until that time sex had not been a subject for general discussion.

Infertility was not open to debate. Married couples desperate to have children did not have access to fertility treatment or counselling services. It was indeed a different world.

Within this different world, however, people still had sex. Unwanted babies were born and those married couples who found they had infertility problems and wanted a family of their own did have one option open to them.

The 1927 Children's Act came as a direct result of the vast problem of unwanted or illegitimate babies born during the Victorian era. The concept of adoption was quite brilliant and certainly provided a way of hiding and dealing with unwanted or illegitimate children.

The Victorian image of an upright, honest and moral society placed the rights of the individual quite firmly with adults. The same ethos was applied to adoption as to the rule of that time that children should be seen and not heard. Illegitimate babies and babies born into families which, for whatever reason could not cope, could be placed, in secret, to married childless couples. This would get rid of a growing problem as well as serve a need.

The adopted parents would, by being issued with a new birth certificate for the child, become the legitimate parents of that baby. All records, if any existed, of a previous identity would be severed and the child would grow up unaware of his or her "past".

Over the next four decades, nothing much changed. Adoptive parents took on children, believing that once legally adopted, the child's origins were safely locked away and confident that no one would ever suspect or know that the child was not theirs.

The birth mother could return to her life without anyone knowing what had happened. It would not be mentioned again and she was assured that her "terrible" secret was safe.

As for the babies, many grew up totally unaware of any difference in their origins. The priority in adoption being given to the adopters, meant that they also had the right to decide whether or not to inform the adopted child of their past.

In theory adoption is a wonderful concept. It is an extraordinary thing to take on, as ones own, a stranger's child. Then to raise, care and be a true parent to that child. It is understandable that the adopted parents needed the security that came with knowing that all links with the child's past were severed.

Adoption is also unique when you realise that not many other animals tolerate this concept. Most species are hostile to another female's offspring; indeed a lion will kill the young of a female with which he wants to mate.

From the late twenties until the early seventies, adopted parents lived secure in the knowledge that "no one would ever find out". It was a family secret; it was not talked about. Similarly, the birth mother was dismissed. No one except the woman herself ever gave thought to the consequences of this very final separation.

One thing overlooked completely were the rights of the adopted child. It was assumed that they had in some way been "saved" from their illegitimacy and given a wonderful new life. That was enough and therefore they were viewed as fortunate individuals who should always be grateful.

By the late sixties, the adopted babies of the thirties, forties and fifties had grown up. Many were unaware of their adoption. Many have, however, claimed to have always felt different, as if they had known, had sensed something. Growing up, however in an atmosphere where a child is forever being told that he/she should be grateful and constantly being reminded of how lucky they are, may explain some of the reasons for feeling different.

Sadly many adults only discovered the truth on the death of an adopted parent, or if they needed their long, full birth certificate for something. Some experiences are even more painful if the truth emerges during a family row.

Children are masters at picking up body language, moods, tension and feelings within a family. They are naturally very inquisitive and like to ask questions. Our minds, our imagination and our ability to question make us unique as the Human Race.

Adoption, as problem solving, as it was for the childless couples and birth mothers, gave rise to a problem that had never been given any thought. It did not allow for the individuality of the adopted child. By the early seventies a small band of adopted adults were openly stating that they wanted to know their origins. The media picked up on this and so began a steady stream of documentaries about adopted people tracing their roots.

The 1975 Children's' Act recognised the growing demand and for the first time, permitted adopted adults, over the age of eighteen, the right to apply for their original birth certificate. The change in law raised many issues and brought with it much controversy.

First it brought fear. Fear by the adopted parents that the children they had raised or were raising would suddenly abandon them for their "real" parents.

Secondly it brought fear to many birth mothers, many who had since married and not mentioned past events. Many had spent years trying to forget. Now their "little secret" could be a rather large adult and there was a quite real and terrifying possibility that this stranger would turn up on the doorstep expecting to be welcomed in by the subsequent family.

What the 1975 Children's Act did was to acknowledge, for the first time, the rights of an adopted person. At eighteen an adoptee could apply for his original birth certificate. In order to obtain that certificate the adoptee would have to be interviewed by a trained social worker. Once the document had been handed over, it was up to the individual to decide whether or not to pursue a search.

There were no teams of people waiting to help adoptees search or to show them how to go about it. The most important thing that the 1975 Children's Act did, however, was to switch the emphasis away from the rights of the adopted parents and to acknowledge the individuality of the adopted person. Thus accepting, for the first time that adopted children were not just items that belonged to their parents. They were people with their own rights.

Since 1975, the door has opened fully. Adoption is not "closed" any more. Priority is given entirely to the child's needs and so the emphasis is on retaining information about birth parents. Adopted parents are no longer able to keep secret their child's origins and in one sense being an adopted parent is more truthfully, being a step-or foster-parent. We have moved from complete secrecy to extreme openness.

For all parties involved, adoption is a difficult and sensitive issue with many possible scenarios. Each situation is different. Each child is different and therefore each adoption should be agreed on the individual's unique needs.

Parents who wish to adopt now have to be prepared to be thoroughly interviewed and questioned on every aspect of their lives. There are many rules and many guidelines to ensure the safety and well being of the child, who, after all is dependent on those people who care for him.

Over the last two decades the media have presented many stories of reunions between adoptees and birth parents. As the stories unfold, it is found that, whatever the outcome of a reunion and however deep an adoptee delves into his birth family, there is always a need to know something. A Lady working within the adoption field once told me that for every person who is adopted, there are twenty relatives, natural and adopted, affected in some way by that adoption.

According to the Office of National Statistics there have been some 877,522 adoption orders made between 1927 and 2001. If you multiply that by the twenty people directly affected emotionally or physically by those adoptions you have around 17550,44 people within this country alone whose lives have been directly touched by adoption.

Between 1982 and 1998 the figures showing adopted adults who have been counselled and therefore made an application for their original birth certificate stand at 53,453. Interestingly out of those people, 33,371 were women and 20,082 men. This does not mean that there were more women adopted just that women are more likely to apply for their original birth certificate. It appears that although men also apply they usually do so at a later age. Perhaps the most obvious reason for this is that women tend to find it easier to discuss emotional issues, where as a man may find it easier after experiencing some life changing event such as the birth of a child or the death of a parent.

Later figures indicate the huge interest we have as a species in our immediate origins.

Across the world the law concerning adoptees, birth parents and their rights vary enormously. In Finland birth parents and adoptees of any age can obtain identifying information. Similarly in Holland, since 1979 adopted persons, over the age of twelve have had the right to information.

New Zealand, although following the British example of allowing adopted adults the right to their original birth certificate, also showed equality by opening up this right to birth parents. This in effect allows a birth mother or father access to disclosing information about the infant they gave up. British law has never allowed this and indeed this is one area that causes much distress to birth parents.

New Zealand, however also introduced a policy to safeguard the rights of individuals that did not wish to be found. This came in the form of a veto, that could be placed on a person's file and basically prevent another individual from accessing their information. The veto expires after ten years, unless the person remembers to renew it. It can also be removed on request of that individual. The effect of this veto is to completely block information and so the adopted person does run the risk of discovering that they are not permitted to any information.

It is interesting that vetoes were only placed by six per cent of birth mothers and two percent of adopted people. The majority of these vetoes were placed in within 1986, the first year in which vetoes were in operation and most have since passed the first ten years without being renewed.

In Australia the rules are modelled on New Zealand. New South Wales is far more open and allows information to both adult adoptees and birth parents. It also, however has made it an offence for an individual to try and make contact with an individual who has registered that they do not wish this.

Because Australia is a federal system, each state or territory has individual differences in the way in which certain aspects of disclosure are handled. In Victoria adopted people have the right to information but only with official intervention. This means that a state official is in charge of arranging meetings and so acts as an official intermediary in all reunions.

In the U.S.A, and Canada, again access to information varies greatly from state or province and so an adopted person's ability to trace a relative is governed by which state they were originally adopted in. Almost a lucky dip in terms of information and the availability of help supplied by that state in arranging contact. For those unlucky souls that find they were given up for adoption in Alabama, they will find that the adoption files have been closed.

However diverse the Federal countries are, we then move on to countries such as Russia and Japan. These countries still maintain complete secrecy over their records, believing that illegitimacy is shameful and should not be discussed by adopted parents or adopted children.

For anyone thinking of searching or struggling with a search, take solace in the knowledge that although in many respects this country is behind in its equality between adopted people and birth parents' rights, it does at least allow for one side to search.

The story I am about to tell began as a "need". A need to know something about the nameless, faceless individuals that created me. I had no idea when I began to search that it would be so complicated, involve so many individuals or that it would take twenty years to complete.

Throughout the search I kept notes and recorded events and feelings that have travelled with me during this time. I have now pieced together this pile of scrap paper and have tried to give an honest account of the bizarre nature of my particular story.

CHAPTER ONE

SPARKS

I do not know when, exactly, I became aware that I wanted to find my natural parents. What I do remember is that one afternoon I was sitting on a bus in Putney, south London when I became quite convinced that a lady who sat opposite me was my "real" mother.

I was ten years old and returning home after swimming training. A woman had climbed on to the bus one stop after me and was so heavily laden with groceries that everyone watched as she stumbled to a seat and then desperately tried to stuff the carrier bags under her feet. Having struggled and having finally found a moments rest she straightened herself and smiled at me. It was a kind, warm smile. A motherly smile.

I returned the smile and she raised her eyebrows as if to say "thank God I made it". I smiled again and then glanced out of the window. It was then that the thought entered my head. I looked at the woman again. Yes, she was about the right age; yes, there was a similarity between us. Same mousy-coloured hair, large blue/green eyes and the same, slightly crooked front tooth. This woman could be my "real" mother.

The thought came with such clarity that within a minute of merely thinking that she could be my real mother, I had total certainty that she was indeed my birth mother and I also believed that she knew it. It was as though, in some way unknown to me until that moment, she had planned our meeting and planned that smile.

The evidence appeared so strong in my mind that I found myself staring at her. This just brought more smiles and I found myself completely delighted at this discovery. Any minute now she would lean over towards me and reveal her true identity. Or she would whisper to me, acknowledging my suspicions.

Instead, I heard the soft "ping" of the bus stopping bell and the woman began to gather the many bags that lay around her feet. After a few moments, she stood and made her way to the exit. The bus stopped and she climbed down onto the pavement. With a swish of folding doors and a soft rumble of an engine, the bus moved away.

I found myself standing on the pavement. The woman was about twenty feet ahead of me, making her way slowly towards a housing estate. I followed her convinced that she was waiting for the right moment to speak with me. Suddenly she stopped and placed the shopping on the ground. This was it. She would turn round and see me. She would be so happy that I had recognised her. She would want to tell me that she was indeed my real mother but because of some tragic events in her life, she had been unable to keep me.

This, of course, did not happen.

After a few seconds she bent down and collected up the bags again. Then she turned and went through a small gate that led to a block of flats. Within a second or two, she had gone, disappearing behind a solid grey exterior that was her home.

As if waking from a dream, I stood, slightly dazed on the pavement outside the flats. I had no idea where I was. I glanced at my watch and realised I would be late for lunch. Quickly I retraced my steps and caught the next bus home.

The experience left me feeling embarrassed at my own impulses. It was so stupid and I realised this. However, for the time I had been in that stranger's company, the belief that I could find my "real" mother had become possible.

My head was filled with new thoughts. All those people out there, all the people I pass, talk to and mix with. Any one of those people could be one of my natural parents. Nothing of huge significance had happened in my life to promote these thoughts. My parents, the ones who were bringing me up had not said anything to make me question my origins. I spent the rest of that day feeling terribly guilty, as though I had double-crossed my parents for even having such thoughts.

This feeling of guilt was made worse because of the feeling of excitement I had experienced whilst following the strange woman. That excitement was so real and so wonderful that I had felt happier than ever before.

It came as a shock to discover that the thought of finding my "real" parents brought with it so much pleasure. It also came as a relief to know that, one-day it might be possible. From that day on, I knew that I would find my birth parents. Adoption, or being adopted did not appear as something to be ashamed of. It was intriguing.

Soon after the bus experience I was asked in school to write an essay titled "My Life". I wrote with great enthusiasm about being adopted, about how, at the age of five I had been told that I had been "specially "picked. It all seemed such an adventure.

On receiving our essays back I was asked to stand and read mine to the class. It did not occur to me once that what I was saying would cause such a reaction from my teacher. At the end of reading I waited. There was complete silence in the class and then the teacher, a rather elderly spinster bellowed out two words. The first was "illegitimate" and the second was "bastard".

Having no knowledge of either of these two words I was bemused. From the gasps that rang out from my classmates I understood instantly that they were not good words, instead they meant something that was not normally talked about.
On arriving home from school that day I went to my mother and asked what "bastard" meant. She did not tell me. Instead she demanded to know where I had heard the word and ordered me never to use it again. Needless to say I didn't, but I did have a dictionary and found it quite easily.
Bastard. N. Illegitimate (child), love child, counterfeit, false, imperfect, impure, irregular, misbegotten, sham, spurious.

I did not know what illegitimate meant, but it sat beside the words "love child". Why was everyone so cross that I was a love child? It seemed a wonderful thing to be. I did not understand.

Things changed, however. I no longer wished to read my essays out loud, for fear of discovering other new words. My classmates on the whole did not change, except one girl who from that day on became quite determined that I should not reach adulthood. Having tried various ways of causing me harm through normal schoolgirl pranks, she then engaged the help of her older brother who supplied her with some "extra special sweeties" as she called them.

I remember being somewhat confused at her sudden friendliness one morning as she offered me a couple of her "sweets". But it was a kind gesture and for about two minutes we became, as little girls do, "best friends". That was the last two minutes that I remember. I do not remember the rest of that day.

I do remember thinking I could fly and finding everything extremely funny. My mother, however, did not find me funny. She did not find my bright red face funny or the fact that I suddenly appeared to have become totally hyperactive and aggressive and so the doctor was called. The little white sweets were not made "of all things nice" they were LSD.

The matter was dealt with and, as always, within our home, never talked about again. Many years later, whilst browsing through "The Adopted Children's Register" at St Catherine's House, I found this girl's name. It is the name directly above mine for children adopted in 1962.

Apart from these two experiences, no one else has ever reacted to my being adopted in such a way. These two things did not make me want to search. The seed was already there, but they did make me start to question things. I realised that the story I had been told at five was not the whole truth but I also understood that it would be impossible to ask questions.

I grew up in a large red-bricked Victorian house in Putney with my adopted mother and father and one brother, adopted from a different family. My parents had met and married relatively late in life. They had wanted children and when my mother, aged forty, found herself to be pregnant, they were delighted. Their only child, a daughter, Amy, was born profoundly mentally and physically handicapped. It was the late 1950's and Society did not have the understanding and acceptance of people with learning difficulties that we do today. Institutions and hospitals were the main homes for these individuals and parents were encouraged to place their "damaged" children within one of them.

My parents had wanted a family. The choice offered to them now, was a cruel one. Either they chose to keep Amy, care for her and give up any chance of being allowed to adopt. Or they agree to place her in full-time care and then try to adopt. They were told that Amy, being so disabled, was unlikely to survive past the age of seven. Not able to have any further children of their own and fast becoming too old to register as prospective adopted parents, my parents reluctantly gave up their daughter, aged four, into full time nursing care and waited to adopt a child.

In 1961 they were offered a baby boy. They accepted and thought that, at last they would have the family they had waited for. In adoption there is a three-month gap between a baby being placed for adoption and the adoption becoming law. The reason is two-fold. Firstly the prospective parents may not "bond" with that child and secondly the birth mother may change her mind and ask for her baby back. My parents kept their new baby son for two and a half months before his birth mother changed her mind. The baby and all the clothes my parents had bought for him were returned to the birth mother.

I was born on the 12th August 1961 and placed into foster care. After a month the Social Services became concerned about my welfare and removed me from my foster mother. It was a Friday in late September and no care could be found. The social worker in charge of my case knew of a couple who had recently lost a baby they were trying to adopt. She called and asked if they would be willing to look after me just for one weekend whilst my future was decided. My future father was to take the call and thankfully, for me, he agreed.

The following Monday my birth mother, agreed to give me up for adoption. Interestingly, I was to find out much later that the social worker, who knew my adopted parents well, asked my natural mother to waiver her right to ask for me back. She even asked her to sign a form agreeing this. My birth mother would have been unaware that this was not a lawful document but it did mean that my future parents, now in their late forties, finally got a baby.

One year after this my parents were offered another baby, this time a boy and with the arrival of Adam, the family was now complete.

I was told of my adoption at a very young age. Shortly after my fifth birthday it was explained to me that instead of coming out of my mother's tummy, I had been "specially picked" by my parents. It was a simple and loving explanation and enough for me to understand that I was somehow different. Not a bad type of difference but one that made me feel special and very much wanted. Adoption did not worry me, on the contrary I found being different from my peers, quite exciting and was often quite vocal about my origins causing many of my little friends to run home and demand to know why they were not "specially picked."

During my childhood, adoption was never "used" as a reason for differences between us. My parents never referred to it at all and it is difficult to say, why, by the time I was ten I had become quite obsessed with the thought of finding my "real" parents.

Children often fall out with their parents; it is part of the normal growing up process. By the time I was ten I had reached puberty, somewhat early. I was five foot six (my height today), weighed in at ten and a half stone and behaved far more like a boy, than the young lady that was hoped for. Very fit I spent nearly all my free time either charging around on a bike or swimming at a local pool.

My parents' now in their late fifties did not have the energy to "play" with me and also did not share my interests. The main difference between us was that I was not and quite obviously never going to be an academic. Already behind at school and always referred to as a late developer (academically), I was far more interested in being active, than studying.

Our home was run on a mixture of routine and orderliness. Each day had its own rules, activities, even its own menu. There were no variations on this. Everything had its own place and its own time. This meant that my parents' own interests in studying and attending events and committee meetings were not disturbed.

Having a disruptive, noisy and rather large ten-year-old charging round did disturb the quiet ambience of our home. My father was frequently away from home on business and my mother, no longer able to use the services of au-pair girls, that she employed when my brother and I were babies, found herself and her way of life interrupted by my frequent and increasing confrontations with her.
My brother was seen as an academic, he was also quiet and unquestioning and what resulted was a complete breakdown in my relationship with my adopted mother.

My parents did find my sheer energy too much to cope with on their own. Although I was not bothered at all by their ages, my mother would often refer to herself as an older mother. Their ages were in fact not the problem. The problem was that having children later in life meant they had already grown accustom to life without children. They had formed their interests and their social circle and these things had become an integral part of their lives.

The other area that undoubtedly was a cause of the, at times, terrible relationship between my mother and myself was the fact that she already had a daughter of her own. Mum has, in recent years, told me that she did not want to adopt a girl. As a mother now myself I can understand this. The thought of having to give up my own child to take on someone else's' and then find that the child you have taken on is so different to all your academic and behavioural expectations, must have been difficult to accept.

What was also so difficult to live with was the fact that Amy did not, as predicted, die at seven years old. Amy lived to reach the age of thirty-three. During that time the ten-year National Health plan saw the closure of many awful Institutions and brought people with learning difficulties out into the community. The Society that had forged the thinking that originally sent Amy away was beginning to condemn this. Parents with handicapped children were beginning to have a voice; allowances and special education facilities were being introduced.

Strangely enough the time I felt closest to my parents was when, once a week we drove to Queen Mary's Hospital, Carlshalton to visit Amy. This was really the only time during the week when, as a family we were together and although these visits always brought a tragic reminder to my mother of what could have been, it was also the only time any real conversations and emotions were shared between us.

When I was eleven my parents found a solution for my outspoken tendencies. Boarding school. An all girls establishment, which catered for the" not so bright" but promised to produce a well-groomed young lady. I was sent away, unwillingly, and this confirmed to me that, not only was I too different from my family but because my brother was allowed to stay at a day school, I believed that I was not wanted anymore.

Within a week of starting boarding school I discovered that nearly one third of the girl's there were adopted children. This proved to me beyond doubt that adopted children could never be fully accepted within their adopted homes. I believed that only the children that fitted in with the ambitions of the adopters' were kept and included.

In reality the truth was quite different. Most children who were given up for adoption during the 40's, 50's and 60's were adopted by middle-class, middle income adopters who could afford private and boarding school fees. Of course, at eleven years old I had no understanding of this and so began a five-year period when, desperate to be back at home I embarked on a mission to get expelled from the school. My academic work was placed a firm second as I proceeded to disobey, challenge and refuse to conform to any authority. It was a peculiar battle that saw me become a different person and one that I did not recognise.

The only two saving graces were firstly that I was able to swim and swim well. That gave me instant popularity amongst my peer group and second was my ability to act and to play the piano, which gave the school another performer who could promote it as a Drama and music school. All the time I was able to swim for the school or play the piano my deteriorating behaviour was overlooked and put down to "needing time to adjust."

Unfortunately my unhappiness and my obsession with being adopted made me vulnerable. If an adult showed me any kindness I would believe that they must be my natural mother. So when one particular member of staff began to show interest in me and offer me personal tuition and guidance, I was drawn unwittingly into a situation of serious sexual and mental abuse that was to continue for the duration of my stay at the school. What I had seen as someone showing me genuine understanding and a little affection was nothing of the kind.

I began writing begging letters home to my mother promising to behave and to conform. Because my parents trusted the school system and because I was now displaying very erratic behaviour they did not realise, and I most certainly could not explain the abuse that was taking place.

I would therefore receive only the weekly typed letter from my mother. It never referred to my pleas just listed their daily activities and any other news from home.

This was a time when I longed to be at home but once there did not feel at home. I dreaded being at school and the result was that an anger grew within me. This anger was not directed at anyone except myself and I found that I could only cope with physical and mental pain by inflicting pain on myself. I would self-harm in order to have something within my control, to focus on.

On a visit home when I was about fifteen years old my mother took me to see a doctor for a minor chronic ailment. I was given some tablets and told the problem would go away. Arriving back at school the matron wanted to know why I needed anti-depressants. I had no idea but this tipped my anger over the edge as I realised that no one was really interested in what I said or felt. Even our own family doctor had made a judgement about me without listening to the facts.

I decided that if my parents and school thought I was depressed it would be best to cure the depression in one go and so swallowed the entire contents of the bottle. How I survived this I will never fully understand as both the school and the doctors insisted that I could not have taken all the pills and must still have some hidden away. I remember finding this hilariously funny. At this time I genuinely did not wish to live and yet it seemed that the only thing every one was interested in was proving me a liar.

I realised that I would never win any argument with either the school or my parents and so spent the next two years surviving on the belief that one-day I would find the people who made me and they would understand me far better. Sometimes this fantasy was turned round and I would become convinced that my real mother was watching me. She was close, like a guardian angel, keeping her eye on me and waiting for the right time to approach me.

Misunderstanding and a lack of communication between my parents and I had resulted in some very distorted reasons for me wishing to find my natural parents. It was, in a way, similar to Chekhov's play, *The Three Sisters*. In the play three sisters survive their lives by believing that when they reached Moscow, "things" will be better. Of course they are not and needless to say, no "real" mother ever stepped towards me during those "surviving" years. I left school a very angry and rather uneducated young woman.

My mother managed to use her contacts and gain me a place a sixth-form college where I was permitted to take A levels. Suddenly free from the restrictions of the microcosm of a Girls' boarding school I was able to come and go as I pleased, dress in whatever manner I liked and for the first time since the age of seven share classes with the opposite sex. So I did what every self-respecting teenager did, took up smoking (big mistake), lost weight, dyed my mousy-brown hair blond, got a small motorbike and found politics and Religion.

I cannot say I found God, but I did find a group of kids my own age that met after church each Sunday. This group brought with it something I had longed for, a real sense of belonging. This feeling of being part of a group of friends, mixing and sharing secrets and romances, good times and bad, it was wonderful.

Quite often I was asked by friends why I was so keen to search for my real parents. I could never find a reason that seemed to justify beginning something that would undoubtedly hurt my adopted parents. It is true that my relationship with my mother was still very fragile but my anger with her dwindled significantly as soon as I established my own set of friends.

A combination of facts and events probably lead me to think about searching I only realised some years later that an adoptee does not require a reason for wanting to know about the past. I am convinced that regardless of the relationship I had with my mother, I would at some stage have wanted to know more about the people who made me. Natural Curiosity and the need to belong are part of our human condition. Wanting to know about the people who created you is natural. It does not require any justification at all.

CHAPTER TWO

THE JOURNEY BEGINS

On the 12th August 1979 my alarm clock rang at 5am. I quickly turned it off so as not to wake the rest of my family. Quietly I slipped on some jeans and a top and collecting a little blue envelope hidden in my desk, crept down the stairs and out through the front door.

The sun, already warming the early morning air brought with it a wonderful sense that this was going to be a good day. I made my way to the end of the road and turned the corner, ahead I could see the bright red post box. Once there I spent a few minutes checking the address on the envelope. Inside it was probably the most important letter I had ever written. I checked the enveloped was firmly sealed and that I had placed the correct stamp on it.

A great sense of excitement filled me. I had waited over four years to be able to post this letter. It had sat hidden in my desk, with today's' date written on the form inside, simply waiting to be posted. Today was my eighteenth birthday, this meant I could marry without my parents' permission, I could buy an alcoholic drink and I could vote. These things did not make me feel like celebrating but being eighteen also meant that in the eyes of the law I was now an adult and there was something else, far more important to me, that I could now do.

Under the 1975 Children's Act, an adopted person, once eighteen years old can, if they wish, legally apply for their original birth certificate. This recognition of my coming of age, was the best birthday present I could ever receive.

Of course I had no idea really of what would happen to my letter other than it was addressed to the Registrar General's office at St. Catherine's House. From what I understood from the application form, this Official would cross-reference my adopted birth certificate with my original one and send all the information to a social worker in my area. When the information was ready I would be sent an appointment. No time scale had been mentioned. It all seemed quite straightforward.

As I let go of the little blue envelope it seemed to me that the four year wait just to post it would soon fade into insignificance and it would only be a short time until I was reunited with my birth mother and father.

At 7am that morning, my father, mother and brother came in to my bedroom to sing "Happy Birthday" to me. I was back in bed and managed to disguise the fact that I had been awake for the last two hours, my thoughts completely consumed with the possibilities of "who "my natural parents might be and what might happen next. By posting that application form for my original birth certificate I had stepped into the unknown; and the nameless, faceless individuals that made me were to change from being just thoughts and fantasies in my head, to real people.

I remember watching my parents as they laughed and talked excitedly about all those things I could now do and as they gave me presents whilst reminiscing about their own eighteenth birthdays. They looked so hopeful for me, as though as an adult I could now achieve things, become someone. Inside me was the thought that I needed to know something about me before I could "be someone." Inside me also, was a tremendous feeling that I was, by my actions that morning, betraying the parents who were now singing to me and giving me wonderful presents.

To say I felt ashamed is true. My father's face, so filled with pride that his daughter was now an adult. My mother and brother, happy to celebrate. I knew that if I was to say anything or to tell them what I had done that morning, it would cause not only upset, but also genuine confusion. They would, as my parents, simply not understand why I needed to know anything.

Part of me wanted to shout out my news. To yell and jump up and down with the excitement of it all. Another part of me wanted to say sorry over and over again and to try and shake off the overwhelming feelings of guilt that filled me as I pretended to share their excitement at my birthday. Most of all I was concerned because we were to go away on our family holiday that day and that meant two weeks of waiting to see if there had been a reply to my letter.

It was, however, some two months later that a reply arrived with an appointment for me to attend the Balham social services office. I was to have a "counselling" session before being allowed to receive my birth certificate. This, I knew, was standard practise for children adopted before 1975. I remember being extremely anxious that I would somehow fail this session and the information would be withheld. In practise, however, the information is a right and therefore the counselling session a formality.

This was my first experience of talking directly to someone about my "need" to know.
The social worker was a woman in her mid-thirties. She was obviously enjoying the fact that she possessed information that I so wanted. Her manner was patronising and ridiculous. "Why did I wish to have my original birth Cert.?" "What was I going to do on receiving it?" I remember her giving me a lecture about "not just turning up on the doorstep of the address on my birth cert," she did not, however, offer any alternative suggestions. I nodded where appropriate and only said what I thought she wanted me to say. Stupid comments like "I just wanted to know my real mother's name." And "Of course I won't upset anyone." It was a ridiculous example of red tape. Finally, when she appeared satisfied she slowly removed a folded birth cert. from her file. Her movements were so slow I wanted to grab it from her but I allowed her to drag the whole episode out because in front of me was something I so dearly wanted.

Finally she opened it and handed it to me. A name immediately caught my attention. A woman's name, my natural mother. "Mary". It was peculiar, almost surreal. I had never considered that a name would be so important, but going from no name to a whole name, proved her existence for me. For the first time I realised that although I had often dreamed of meeting her, I had not really thought of her as a having her own identity. This was exciting and extremely emotional. I found myself repeating her name over and over. "Mary Brown, My mother's name is Mary Brown."

Under her name was the address for Mary at the time I was born. The excitement of this was almost too much. I knew the road. Worple Road, Wimbledon. How bizarre to think that we had both walked down this road several times. We may have even passed one another. It was tantalising.

The next thing I noticed came as a shock. Under Father's name was a line that just ran diagonally across the space.

"Oh, I should explain," said the social worker. "Father's do not have to be named. Only the mother is responsible for the birth.
This was a disappointment. What did it mean? Perhaps he had not known about my birth or perhaps Mary had not known who the father was?

"Is this it?" I enquired. The social worker explained that I should now apply for my social service and court records from the time of my adoption. This could be arranged for me and again, when the information was gathered I would be sent an appointment.

The day after receiving my original Birth Certificate, I again felt a deep sense of guilt at possessing the name of my birth mother. This information alone seemed almost a betrayal of my adopted parent's love. One part of me enjoyed the knowing and the fact that this information was mine. It belonged to me, and was about me. The other half of me watched my parents carefully, in case they suspected anything, in case they wondered why I appeared so preoccupied. I knew I would have to tell them soon.

I had only ever raised the subject of adoption once before. I was sixteen at the time and it was a Saturday. Dad and I were going alone to visit Amy. I remember thinking it would be the only opportunity to speak with him about the matter and so on our way home I asked him if he knew anything about my past. To my surprise dad said that he was surprised that I had not asked him any questions before. It seemed that my fear of breaching the subject was unfounded, as dad appeared only too happy to talk about it. He did not, however, know very much. Just that he thought my birth father had been a diplomat and my birth mother a young unmarried secretary.

At that time I still had two years to wait before being allowed my Birth Certificate. Now, in possession of my natural mother's name and an old address, for her, it seemed it would be only be a matter of days before I found her.

I decided that it would be best to inform my parents that I was actively searching. The guilt I felt at secretly beginning the search was growing daily with the possibility that I would make contact with Mary and then have to tell my parents after the event. Somehow that seemed worse, although the thought of telling them at all filled me with dread. I remember waiting until they had settled in front of the television one evening and then asking them if I could speak with them. What to say? How to put it without causing pain? I did not know where to begin and so in a rather abrupt manner just informed them, that I thought they had the right to know I was searching.

There was the awful yet predictable silence from mum who did not look at me but continued to stare ahead at the television. Dad looked upset but said that he knew I wanted to search and so I should do what I thought was right. Whenever my parents have said that I should do what I feel is right I have taken that to be their way of saying that they do not feel that what I am doing is right but are not going to make that judgement. It is like being given a chance to re-think and come up with a more appropriate plan of action. In this case I took it that Dad did not understand why I should need to search but it was my decision and I should understand this.

I do not know exactly how I thought they would react, in many ways if they had become angry I would at least have been able to argue my case with them. The silence and their long faces I found very disturbing and all I felt was ashamed to have told them.

I was feeling this guilt quite intensely because I thought I would soon be reunited with my birth parents. This feeling of anticipation was making me very anxious and the last thing I wanted was for my parents to discover what I was doing from one of my friends. I also thought that once I had told them I would feel better about it all, that the "air" would be cleared and it would be easy to go forward. I did not realise that in many ways telling my parents only made me feel even more guilty as now when I talked with them or sat with them I knew that they were struggling to understand my actions and their unhappiness showed through the uneasy silences between us.

Worple Road is just a bus journey away from our house. All the time I sat on the bus I wondered, this time for real whether any of the women on the bus might be Mary. Climbing down and stepping off the bus I turned the corner from the main high street in Wimbledon and was in Worple Road. Each step I took towards the house was wonderful, as I knew that Mary would have walked along this road. It was so exciting to think that I was somewhere she had actually been. It made her real.

The house was a large Victorian dwelling. Bay windows on the ground and first floor. I walked up the driveway and rang the bell. A man answered and I asked whether he knew a Mary Brown. He told me the house was now divided into six flats and he knew of no one by that name. The door closed.

The excitement and the hope of finding her there vanished in an instant. The words of the social worker lecturing me about not just" turning up at an address "filled my head with thoughts of what I would have done if Mary had answered the door? It was the first time I had given any real thought to that possibility. I found I was actually relieved that she wasn't there and could not believe my stupidity at just marching right up to the door.

To live with the thought of finding my natural mother or father was like a dream with a happy ending. That, however, is the nature of dreams or fantasies, about people who are not real. If Mary Brown had answered the door I have no idea what I would have done or said, but it could (and from the knowledge I now have, would) have caused harm. This experience was probably an invaluable lesson in taming my totally impulsive nature. I was forced, rightly, to think about all the possible scenarios that could have happened if I had stood face to face with my natural mother on that doorstep.

Instead, I decided to wait patiently, for the social service and court records to be found.

CHAPTER THREE

THE BREAKTHOUGH

Social Service and Court Records are a compilation of information gathered at the time of a child's adoption. They contain information about the birth mother and father and often include the reasons why a baby is being given up for adoption. Adoption records have to be kept for 75 years and nowadays these files are often transposed onto microfilm but I was fortunate enough to still have a traditional, if not rather dog-eared, folder.

The reason that it was a blessing that my file had not be put onto microfilm only became apparent the second time I visited the Social Service Department which held them.

My first visit had been in December 1979, some two months after receiving my birth certificate. I knew, from my Birth Certificate that my original name, the one Mary gave me at birth was Ingrid. On arriving at Kingston Social Services to read my records I was presented with a file marked "Patricia". This name was alien to me, who on earth was Patricia? After some confusion, not only from me but the social worker dealing with my enquiry it was discovered that whilst in the care of a foster mother I had been given the name Patricia.

It was quite comical really to think that within the first six weeks of my life I had been called Ingrid by one person, Patricia by another and then, finally, Francesca, the name my adopted parents chose for me.

I had tried to remind myself, through the sheer excitement of it all, not to expect too much information. The disappointment at not having a birth father's name on my original birth certificate made me a little more cautious this time. This time the social worker did not hover over the information and there were no lectures about my use of the information I was about to receive. The folder was handed to me and I opened it. Immediately a new name appeared. Orlando, my birth father's name. The last letter of his surname however had been altered and could be one of three different surnames. At this point I had no knowledge how difficult this tiny error would make my forthcoming search I was just delighted to know that I had a named birth father.

The Records stated that my birth mother, Mary was twenty-three, unmarried and Norwegian. In 1961, at the time of my birth, she was working as a Clerk in London. My birth father, Orlando was thirty-seven, married, but hoping for a divorce. He was German and working on contract to the Foreign Office, under the Official Secrets Act. This I was told enabled him to avoid giving too many details about himself.

The story they gave for my adoption was that because Orlando's divorce was not through yet, they felt it was best if I was given up. Mary was planning, after my birth, to return to Norway to care for her sick and elderly mother.

It seemed to me that I was now completely filled with information, everything I had wanted to know, it was magical. Each little extra snippet of information brought Mary and Orlando a little more to life and there was a real sense that this was, after all, a tragic love story.

From quite a young age I liked the notion of being a "love Child", born to two people so desperately in love and yet, for some reason, unable to keep me. My fantasies did not involve them being well known or wealthy; it just had a theme of romantic tragedy. I think the reason this fantasy appealed so much was because that ruled out the image of being an "unwanted" pregnancy and therefore I had only been given up due to circumstances. There was always the exciting thought that, at any point, Mary and Orlando's circumstances could change and they would, quite naturally want to find me.

This, of course, was simply a most wonderful coping strategy and one that allowed me to deny any thoughts that there could possibly be other reasons for my adoption.

The fact that Mary was Norwegian and Orlando was German did come as a surprise, I had never thought of these people being anything other than British. My adopted father was originally German and I wondered if Orlando knew this. Perhaps they knew more about my adopted parents and my life than I realised; perhaps it was all a coincidence? Whatever, the information was enlightening.

On arriving home that day I realised that in my haste to leave the Social Services and phone all my friends with my news, I had managed to leave behind my Birth Certificate. I wrote a letter to thank the social worker for the interview and to ask if she could send my certificate back to me.

At the same time I began writing letters. I did not think there was much point trying to find their Birth Certificates, as being born outside the U.K. and indeed not English; their records would not be here. Instead I wrote to the German Records office, The Norwegian Embassy, the German Embassy and the Foreign Office.

Each time I received a reply, the excitement was immediately thwarted by the lack of information existing on my birth parents. I was writing letters daily to any relevant government office that might just have some record of them, but it did not bring any information. No one, it seemed had ever heard of either Orlando or Mary.

After about nine months and still at a point of having received no information on my birth parents, I felt a need to look at my adoption file again, just in case I had missed some vital information. My Birth Certificate had not been returned and so that gave me a good excuse to contact the Kingston Social Services and make another appointment.

This appointment was to change my search and indeed enrich my life with something that I could never have envisaged. I arrived, as usual, early at Kingston and was met by the same social worker. She was quite agitated and most apologetic. She said that they had now found ALL my records. All my records? I thought I had seen them all. She was sorry but it appeared I had two files and had only been shown one.

I was taken into a side room and there on the table were two thick files. One marked Patricia; this one I had seen and another marked

Ingrid Brown. The social Worker then said she would leave me alone whilst I looked through them.

On opening the file marked Ingrid a letter fell out. It was dated 7th March 1963, one and a half years after my birth. I began to read the neat, but childlike handwriting. It was a letter written by Mary, my birth mother. It told that she had just given birth to a baby boy and wanted him to be adopted by the same family that had adopted me. Orlando was named, again, as the father.

My immediate reaction was to burst into tears. I don't really know why, but tears just poured out. There was a peculiar sensation of something going terribly wrong. Suddenly I was thrown into a new unknown territory, one that involved more than just my own existence. It was quite simply the reality that I was not alone. Another person, just like me, existed out there. A man, now in his early twenties, who may or may not know about me, who may or may not be searching and who was my brother, my full blood brother.

What had happened to this baby? Why did my adopted parents not adopt him? Where did he go? It was obvious from Mary's letter that she was still unable to marry Orlando and therefore would also have to give this baby up. It seemed so sad and yet I also felt a completely new emotion, relief. Relief, that I was not alone.

I thought of my adopted brother Adam. We were close and shared thoughts and feelings over our adoptions. He did not wish to trace his natural parents, felt that it was wrong to do this when we already had good parents. I admired this, saw it as very honourable and it made me feel worse about searching. Adam, it appeared was able to put aside his own needs in order to protect our adopted parent's feelings. I was not and this very much added to my guilt. I wondered what Adam would think if I told him that I had a brother. I had never considered anything like this.

There was a time when I was very young and had done something naughty I would believe I was a twin and that I had been given away for my bad behaviour but this was again, just a fantasy and one that had only lasted a few years. It had been given up in preference for being a tragic couples "love baby". Now, suddenly, I was one of two lost "love babies".

Like following complete strangers and being absorbed at the thought that they were truly my natural parents, the fantasy always ended when the person was out of sight. Now a small part of me began to accept the thought that I was not exactly a "love-child". I knew, whilst reading Mary's letter that the birth of this baby, she had called Karl, was a sign that I may have to accept a new, not so pleasant truth about my birth.

The file also contained letters written by Mary to a social worker, for up to three years after my adoption. In them she requests photographs of me. Repeatedly says she is sorry for asking but would it be possible to have some pictures. I noted that all the enquiries were made on or around the time of my birthday and realised how hard it must have been to have to remember each year, the babies she gave up. I wondered if the pain ever went?

The social worker returned and found me sobbing whilst, at the same time, smiling at the news. She apologised again for not having known about the second file and then delighted with me at the discovery of a brother. She then explained that at the time of my adoption the Law required that no contact be made between the natural mother or father and the adopted parents. "Closed" adoption meant exactly that. Once legal, all ties with any "past" were severed forever. The birth of a second child and the possibility of this child being offered to my parents was, at that time, impossible.

Adam, the brother I grew up with, was born in October 1962 and so would have already been adopted by my parents by the time Karl was born. My adopted parents in later years were to tell me that if they had known of a second child, they probably would have adopted him. That however would have affected Adam's life and created a totally unbalanced sibling structure within our family.

In fairness to the legislation of the day, the way in which adoption was handled then did not incorporate the option of being able to offer a later born sibling to the same adopters. This was probably because most women only went through one accidental pregnancy, and so Karl had been placed for adoption with another couple.

Looking at Mary's letter I saw that Karl had been born in Bolton, Lancashire. Maybe Mary did not bring him back to London, as she planned, maybe he was adopted in Lancashire. I now felt a deep need to find this brother and to meet him.

Here began a new problem. British Law does not recognise the rights of adopted siblings. It is not equipped for the possibility of unmarried couples giving up more than one baby and therefore no legislation exists to enable an adopted adult to trace another adopted sibling. Having no guideline meant that, in effect I had no automatic rights to information about Karl. I could, however, from the information in Mary's letter now obtain Karl's birth certificate and that would, at least show that we were blood related. I also wanted to see if Karl's Birth Certificate included Orlando's name or whether, like with mine, Orlando had managed to escape being named on this birth certificate too.

It was not hard to find an entry for Karl at St Catherine's house. Again, no father's name appeared but it was great to have documented proof of my brother's existence.

My enquiries about Mary and Orlando were still getting nowhere and by 1984 having written well over one hundred letters to every department and government office within this country, Norway and Germany, I was getting really stuck. It did not matter which surname I tried for Orlando, none were recognised. By all accounts it appeared that neither individual had been born in Germany or Norway. The only remaining address for Mary was one that she used when writing to the Social services to ask for photos of me. This was another London address. Kingly Street, very close to Liberty's in London.

I wrote to the address and was informed that this was, during the early sixties, a "mailing" address. It seemed strange that Mary should go to such lengths not to give out her real address. I was also becoming very despondent about the way in which no help is offered to adopted adults who are trying to trace their birth families. Although the children's Act allows adults to obtain their original Birth Certificate, no provision is actually made to help people search. There were a few people who would search for you at a price and I even hired the services of a Private Investigator, who charged me several hundred pounds to confirm that there was no information about Mary and Orlando.

Throughout the search I tried whatever ideas came into my head. Not having any prior knowledge of how to trace someone, it took a long while before I understood how to look through records. In a moment of madness I even hired the services of a "psychic" who, although unable to find any link with a living or dead natural relative did say that my spiritual guide was dressed in Lederhosen? It was good that Ben, my future husband, had a good sense of humour. It is also good that Ben is an immensely patient person as my sudden and frequently (in my opinion) "brilliant ideas" on searching have, over the years, brought with them some very trying moments. Searching can, at times be extraordinarily frustrating. Sending an enquiring letter off brought with it the excitement of possibilities, maybe this time a small but significant piece of information would be found, there was always the chance and the days spent waiting for a reply where always filled with hope.

Each disappointing reply immediately ate into my optimism and brought frustrations and depression with the effect of making me want to give up searching altogether. Quite often after receiving a batch of negative answers I would find that for a while I would not wish to continue and engross myself instead in my life, and my relationship with Ben. Always though, whether it was just a few weeks or a few months something would spur the interest on again. Sometimes a television programme on adoption or a radio interview with an adopted person would inspire me but more often than not it would be just noticing a stranger and finding I was yet again looking for similarities between us. Having Ben supporting me emotionally with his easygoing and always calm manner certainly helped to keep my impulsive actions and mood swings in perspective.

In 1983, I was twenty-two and living at home with my parents in Putney whilst working as a lifeguard at a local swimming pool. I had been going out with Ben for two years. In May that year I found myself pregnant. This came, as a total shock as I was taking the pill and believed this sort of thing would not happen to me. I thought of Mary falling pregnant with me at exactly the same age. I thought of my adopted parents and what they would say and realised that the fear of being unmarried and falling pregnant still remained. There was no way I could tell my adopted parents. I also did not want Ben to have to marry me.

I knew that I loved him and would marry him if he asked but believed it should be without any persuasion. I also wondered if Ben might think that I had become pregnant on purpose, in order that he would marry me. The thoughts all swirled around and this brought with it a new understanding of how easy it is to judge someone who has made a mistake. I could, for the first time understand why Mary could not keep me. I did not, however have her courage and chose, instead, to have an abortion. This action was, I know, the coward's way out of not having face my parents or make Ben feel awkward. Most of all I chose this route because I did not want to repeat history and give up my own baby. Unfortunately, the abortion was performed at a less than hygienic clinic and afterwards I became quite seriously ill. By late 1984 I had been in hospital two further times and was now, at the age of twenty-three told it would be impossible for me to have any more children.

My reasons for tracing my natural family now changed. I felt as though I was a spare cog in a wheel. I had no connection to my past and was told I would produce no future. There was a real sense of being without history and belonging. Thankfully Ben stuck with me and simply would not accept the possibility of us not having future children.

Ben's family came as a complete revelation to me. So many brothers and sisters with parents who loved nothing more than their adult children around them. Their home was always filled with laughter and the smell of his mother's marvellous cooking. Ben's mother adored being a mother and spent each working hour of the day looking after her children.

Coming from a background where everything had its own time and place and where emotions were not expressed openly, I found Ben's family, quite alarming. Here there were no rules about where you sat, when you ate or what cup, plate or space you occupied. Bodies, namely Ben's siblings rose when they liked, ate when they liked and spent hours together, sharing their news and problems. It was wonderful but it reinforced my feelings of not having my own family, in any sense.

Added to this was Ben's rich family history. Ben has a great sense of pride in his family history and, as a family they had managed to document their history back to the Vikings. They spent time together discussing various family members; enjoying listening to each other's stories and life-events. Keeping ties and links with other family members all enforced their closeness as a family unit. This symbolised to me a real family with a real sense of history and belonging. Family members were genuinely interested in each other's lives and well being. There were strong, close bonds within his family and they unconditionally welcomed me into their home. They did not judge me by my lack of academic achievements or make any criticisms about my appearance. Instead they were interested in me as an individual and this I found quite extraordinary.

Although I loved my parents and brother my upbringing and home life was far removed from this relaxed and jolly home. I would spend meal times watching Ben's family as they laughed, all talking and sharing and listening to each other. It was so easy and natural and I wondered if this was because they all came from, and shared the same genetic material. It is true that there is a strong physical likeness between many of his family members, especially the eyes, but it was their personalities that blended together so well.

Inherited traits and learned behaviour, the old nature or nurture issue is a subject area always questioned. Was this what I was looking for? A natural family closeness that goes with belonging to the same "tribe", the same "blood". Were most families like this? I did not know but after a few months of being somewhat overwhelmed by the spontaneous affection shown to me by this family, I realised that I was accepted by them as a person in my own right and this I found inspiring.

To say I envied the wholesome qualities this family possessed is true, Their way of life as a strong family unit brought meaning and purpose, not only for those within the nest but for all the future generations.

Ben's parents were Ex-pats. Having spent most of the previous twenty years in the South Pacific. Ben, his two brothers and sister had not actually spent much time together as they had all attended boarding schools in England only to be reunited during the holidays. Their separation from each other had not distanced them from each other because right at the core of the family was a grandmother and an aunt.

These two ladies, living in a humble bungalow in Dorset provided the communication post between all the members of Ben's family ensuring that wherever and whatever everyone was doing, it was known about and shared. With regular family get-togethers at the bungalow; the house itself has, over the years become the "foundation stone" of this family and the one thing that never changes.

Stability, a sense of belonging and delight in spending precious time together has given Ben's family something unique and something that is fundamentally missing from many adopted people's lives.

I began to wonder about my ancestors, not only the immediate problem of locating my natural mother and father, but their ancestry. It would be interesting to know more, far more.

I decided, as the search for my birth parents seemed to be going nowhere I would concentrate on finding my brother, Karl and so, armed with his original birth certificate I travelled to Bolton, Lancashire, where he was born.

Normally Ben came with me to help me search, but this time he was unable to and so I took a long-suffering, sympathetic friend. On reaching the town of Bolton we headed for the Social Service Department. On arriving I explained to an official that I believed my brother had been adopted in Lancashire and could he check to see if they held his adoption records.

A social worker, Mr Thompson, appeared and took the copy of Karl's birth certificate, asking whether we would like to return in one week! Impossible I told him. We had only come up for the day and would like the information in one hour. Thankfully he seemed to understand the "desperate" tone in my voice and agreed to see if he could find out anything.

My friend and I then took a bus from Bolton town centre in the direction of the address given for Mary at the time of Karl's birth. We were looking for Ivy Bank Road. It was not hard to find. Again I had the same feelings as in Wimbledon, when walking along a road that Mary must have known. It gave me the feeling of being very close to her. It didn't matter that she would have walked that street some twenty years before, I could imagine her, pregnant, probably alone and frightened.

We reached Number eleven Ivy Bank Road and a surge of excitement grew within me as I contemplated the possibility of Mary still living at Number twelve. No sooner had we passed number eleven we found we were at number thirteen. Where was twelve? We retraced our steps but could not find it. Then we crossed the road and checked all the house numbers on that side. There appeared to be no Number 12.

In the end we resorted to knocking on doors for information. At one house a lady answered and invited us in. We spent an hour being served tea and biscuits by a delightful lady who informed us that there was never a number twelve! She knew all the people who had ever lived in that street and had never heard of Mary Brown. She suggested we call at a little church at the end of the road to check for marriages in the parish records.

The vicar was at the church and once we had explained the problem he was very enthusiastic about opening up the parish records. Fascinating as they were, they held no answers. We returned to the Social services in Bolton town centre slightly confused as to why Mary would put an address on a Birth Certificate, which did not exist. One thing was certain and that was that either Mary or Orlando must have known the area extremely well to know about the missing Number in Ivy Bank Road. I think it was at this point that I realised that someone had worked very hard to make sure that Mary and Orlando would not be found.

On our return to the Social Services office, Mr Thompson said that he did indeed have Karl' records, but I was not allowed to read or have any of the information that was contained in them. Even though I was Karl's sibling I was not entitled to know anything about his adoption. Apart from the total frustration I felt at this point, I did now know that Karl had been adopted in Lancashire, probably in Bolton, as his records where still there and that, at least, narrowed the area of my search.

What to do? I did not know. Being so close to knowing about Karl and yet not allowed the information was exasperating. On returning home I wrote to Mr Thompson and thanked him for seeing me, I asked him whether there was anything else he could or would tell me.

The letter Mr Thompson wrote back to me, was, I think the most frustrating letter I ever received during this whole search. Mr Thompson was obviously a person who wanted to help me find Karl but he was limited by the lack of legislation guidelines over siblings and their rights. Even my request that the Social Services contact Karl's adopted parents, on my behalf, was denied. Instead Mr Brown wrote to let me know that the family who adopted Karl still lived at the same address in Bolton, but of course I was not allowed to have that address, or the family name.

I have, for most of this search tried to be quite careful about making approaches. Always remembering marching straight up to the door at Worple Road and the stupidity of this action. But this non-disclosing information from Mr Thompson just made me cross.

If I had trained as a social worker I would have been able to access this information with out anyone's knowledge. It was as though adoption agencies and the social services were playing God with people's lives. Who decided which relatives a person is entitled to know? Surely that is not a decision anyone can make, as the implications are dreadful. It appeared to me that bureaucracy and small-minds were to shape whether or not I ever found my brother.

Mr Thompson wanted me to understand that this decision was made in my brother's best interests. That he was protected because he may not know of his adoption and the "closed" adoption theory was vital for the best interest of the child.

If Karl were still a child, then I would be in total agreement. We were; however, discussing a twenty three-year old man, who, I felt had the right to make his own decisions about his life and his family. It is interesting how often, when referring to tracing siblings it is as though you are tracing a baby or a young child. It seems to me that the government when drawing up their white papers on adoption often forget that the baby adopted before 1975, has grown up and is now very much an adult.

If the Law was not going to provide a decent way in which people in my situation could find their siblings then being "sensitive" about this issue was going to become increasingly difficult as I would have to resort to a more public ways of making contact.

I phoned *The Bolton Evening News* and asked if they would be willing to place an advertisement in their paper for my brother. Obviously I still was not allowed his adopted name, but if he was searching and had obtained his original Birth Certificate then he would be aware that his original name was Karl Brown.

The paper agreed.

CHAPTER FOUR

THE FIRST REUNION

It was now 1986 and I was living with Ben in Windsor. We owned a small terraced cottage just on the outskirts of town. I worked for the Social Services, teaching adults with learning difficulties at a Day Centre in Slough. My day began at 7.30am and so I always missed the morning post.

I had placed an advertisement in *The Bolton Evening News* that read:
"Does anyone know the whereabouts of Karl Brown born 7 March 1963 and placed for adoption in the Bolton area? His sister is looking for him."

Ben was convinced that every weirdo and lunatic would reply. I spent four days following the publication of the advertisement terrified that on my return from work at 4.30pm there would be a sack of mail at the door, filled with letters from strange men all claiming to be my brother. By the fifth day of no post whatsoever, not even a bill, I returned home the next day to be greeted with just one letter waiting on the doormat.

I knew, before opening it that it was from Karl. It had taken over four years to get to this moment. Four years of trying, without any help, to find my brother. I stepped over the letter and went to the kitchen. I lit a cigarette and put the kettle on. For a few minutes I just stood there. There was no hurry to open it; I knew this search was over. I could not, however allow myself to believe that the letter would contain good news. I was certain that it would be a letter telling me to mind my own business or just letting me know how insensitive the advertisement had been.

By the time I picked up the white envelope I was physically shaking so much I had to put it down again and wait a little longer. There was, however, no need for my anxiety. The letter inside was short. The man writing just wanted to let me know that Karl Brown had been his birth name and that he believed he was my brother.

Could I call him, after six in the evening, to arrange a meeting? It was signed John.

I am not sure whether the tears that rolled down my face and drenched the little letter where from excitement or relief, at last I had made contact with one member of my natural family.

When Ben arrived home from work, he did not need to ask me what was going on, he knew instantly and took the soggy letter from my hands. Ben did not say anything, just smiled. It was a smile that lasted all evening.

At six 0' clock that evening, I found I couldn't make the call. It was simply too terrifying and again I had the feeling that John may not really want this contact. Ben called the number for me and began to speak with John. Within a few seconds Ben was laughing and joking with this man and then Ben handed the phone to me. For quite sometime John and I could only utter the word "hello". We must have said "hello" to each other, over twenty times and each time brought with it a laugh. John had a quiet soft Lancashire accent and after our long initial inability to speak to one another I found him chatty and just as thrilled as I was to have finally made contact.

John said that his adopted father had read the advertisement. Knowing that John had a sister and remembering his original name, he realised it was John and told him. Unknown to his adopted father, John had already started searching for his birth mother and father but was unaware that he had a sister. He also had reached a dead-end in his search for birth parents and so this was great news.

We quickly agreed that he would come down the next weekend. I placed the phone down and again burst into tears whilst trying to babble my way through the information we had shared. Ben continued to smile. Then it hit me. John was coming on Friday. That was only two days away!

At this moment I was no longer on my own. I felt as though I was stepping onto a bridge that crossed a river between my two identities. On one side, the side I was leaving was the identity that was given to me at my adoption. On the other was the identity I would have known if I had not been adopted. I knew that John was also stepping on to his own bridge, which would lead him to the same unknown area as me. It was immensely exciting, but also, frightening, as it meant that all my fantasies and thoughts would undoubtedly change. Whatever the outcome of this reunion, there would be no turning back. I was not sure what exactly I was looking for in John, but knew that I would, simply by seeing him know more about myself. I also knew the same applied to John and that there was a chance we might not like each other. This thought terrified me more than anything.

I had gone into work that Friday morning, but was sent home due to being incapable of acting in any rational way. I was just a nervous wreck. The excitement of meeting my brother was unbearable; it made me feel sick. When anyone spoke to me I would either burst into tears or burst out laughing. I could not concentrate on anything.

Having smoked more cigarettes than in the entire time I had been smoking I just did not know what to do with myself. It was only eleven o'clock in the morning, the house was so clean I did not recognise it and John was not expected until six that evening. Suddenly there was a knock at the door and I jumped with fright. My God, I thought. He's early, but it wasn't him. Instead it was my neighbour who knew what was happening that day and thought I might like her company and a drink to calm my nerves. I do not drink as I react to alcohol very quickly but my neighbour, however was most insistent that I should calm down, after all, she kept reminding me, what would John think to arriving to find someone who was unable to speak through nerves. I had a drink. It was now 2pm.

At six o'clock sharp there was a knock at the door. Through the half-glazed window I could make out the shape of a man. A very tall man. I opened the door. In front of me stood John. Six foot six inches tall, very skinny with cropped hair and a bushy moustache.

To say I had never envisaged this moment was true. It only dawned on me as I opened the door that I didn't know how to greet him. It was also true that I was, thanks to my neighbour now completely drunk and therefore passed caring about niceties. So John, having driven for seven hours from Lancashire to meet his long lost sister was not greeted with a kiss, but a five-foot, six inched, rather drunk female who was only capable of insisting that "he must need a toilet after such a long journey!"

Thankfully, John is a kind man and wisely chose to ignore my enquiries about his bladder. He also managed, quite calmly to ignore me, as I stood dumb-founded in his presence. I had waited so long to be reunited with one of my birth relatives I had never given thought to what I would do when it happened. Nobody ever gives you the knowledge of how to greet a complete stranger who is actually a close blood relative. Not only with this first and most wonderful reunion, but at all subsequent meetings, I have found there is a moment of complete uncertainty as to how to greet a natural relative. On the television, in films and in the imagination, there is the assumption that you embrace, that your emotions take over, but it is not the case. It is actually one of the most awkward greetings to make.

My neighbour, sensing this was one of those being alone moments, promptly apologised to John for "getting me into a state" and left. John found the kettle in the kitchen and somehow I managed to pull myself together to make him a cup of coffee.

The first thing that struck me when I opened the door was his height. When we had talked over the phone he had asked if I was tall and I had said I was of average height, at five foot six inches. It is true that I had as a child grown fast and in fact was this height by the age of ten but I had then stopped growing. John had told me he was tall, but in our little cottage, he was like a giant. Not only was he tall, but thin. Painfully thin and pale, reminding me of the pictures of people who survived the concentration camps. His eyes were large like mine, but blue. A piercing light blue. He had brown hair cut severely in army style and a thick moustache that looked awkward on his long thin face.

I found as the evening went on our conversation was primarily concerned with physical similarities and differences between us. It is, as I have found since with all reunions, something that is of great importance to adopted people. To find similar features is reassuring, it gives proof that two people belong to the same "set", it reinforces the fact that you are related. The fact that, at first glance, John and I did not seem to resemble each other at all was mainly due to his height, which was, for me something quite unexpected. I am not sure how I was expecting John to look but if I had been sitting on a bus and had to pick one person as being my natural relative I certainly would not have picked John.

What we both did have in common however is the ability to chat and chat we did. As night moved into early morning it was as though we were trying to catch up on twenty-five years of history in a night. An impossible task and one that Ben survived until about 3am when he finally gave up and went to bed, leaving us to talk more. Although we could not see similarities between us immediately as time went on, they appeared through our interests in music and sports and also through our habits. Both John and I smoke. Both of us do not drink (neighbours pending) and both of us bite our nails, not just a little nibble from time to time but we both fully massacre any chance of normal nail growth.

We both play the piano; John has passed all grades and is able to teach. We both like to compose pieces for the piano and when, the next morning we played each other pieces that we had made up, we were amazed at just how similar they were. Some things seemed uncanny, it was odd to think of this person, being so similar in some ways and yet living his life completely differently and still the genes that had been passed down had created likenesses of a kind I had not imagined.

What is conditioned into a person and what is inherited was definitely challenged by this meeting but with only two individuals from one family a scientist could argue that our similarities were purely coincidence.

The other thing that immediately bonded us was the shared need to find our natural parents.

John was adopted as a baby. His adoption had been arranged before Mary left the maternity hospital. Like me, John's adopted parents were older than average and they had one other adopted child, a girl. From an early age John had not felt part of his adopted family. Unlike me he was not told of his adoption, instead constantly reminded how "lucky" he was, without understanding why. His relationship with his sister was, to say the least, difficult. At family gatherings aunts, uncles and other family relations would constantly remind him of his good fortune and yet, apart from feeling different he did not know why.

The knowledge that he was adopted came during a family row. This is the worst way for a person to discover something like this. For years his parents had not told him. They were not obliged to and yet reference had been made to his different character and personality throughout his life. The row was between John and his sister. The news came as a total shock.

It is understandable that John was angry about this news and even angrier that no one had told him and yet all the adopted family relatives knew. It was the family secret about him that only he did not know. This explained to John the reasons why it would have been impossible for him to ever be fully accepted by his adopted family when young. The row was the final straw and shortly afterwards, with the relationship between John and his adopted parents reaching rock bottom, John left to join the army.

John did not have any more contact with his parents for a year until he was told that his adopted mother had been fatally injured crossing a road close to their home. Out of all the members of his family, he was closest to his mother and her death has taken years for him to come to terms with.

As John spoke about his life I realised that he was a man consumed with anger. His height alone gave him a certain presence but he was so thin with dark shadows under his eyes and he was living off a huge amount of physical energy and emotion. John told me that he had been accepted for Police training and would begin that soon. There was desperation about him, so much pain. It was as though this was the first time in his life he had spoken with someone who not only understood his pain, but also shared the excitement and joy at finding a natural relative.

During the next day we got out all our information in our social service records and read through it. With in a few minutes we noticed that although Mary and Orlando had given similar information out at the time of our adoptions, there were differences that just didn't make sense.

This came as a bit of a shock. The notion that John and I were "loved accidents" was seriously challenged by the fact that both Mary and Orlando were obviously trying to cover up their identities. It posed the question.... why? It also made me realise that they may never wish to be found by us.

In John's adoption file, Mary had mentioned her father's name, Archibald Brown. She stated that he was dead but had owned a Newsagent and Tobacconist shop. She also mentioned her mother's maiden name. This gave me the Norwegian connection.

As we talked it became clear that we had followed almost an identical path in our searches. It was extraordinary as two years earlier we had both made enquiries about Orlando to the same man at the same German office in Berlin. Our letters must have landed on Herr Schneider's desk almost on the same day and yet this man had chosen not to make a connection.

Words are sometimes not enough to describe just how important it is for an adopted person to feel that they have found someone that they can identify with. The weekend with John went too fast. It was terrible saying goodbye to him. I wanted to keep him with me, to get to know him and to try to share all those missed years. There was so much to learn about him.

I thought of what it would have been like to grow up with John. To have had him as a brother from the very beginning. It made me sad to think that, although we are siblings, we are strangers and do not have the natural bond that goes with having a "history" together.

The difference in meeting John from the reunions between birth parents and children, is that, being siblings, we are on equal terms. Our reunion would cause little offence to any people involved in our adoptions. In fact my adopted parents were delighted. This came as a surprise to me until I realised that siblings do not present the same threat to an adopted parent as that of a birth mother or father.

My parents' reaction to my reunion with John came as a welcome surprise. They found it wonderful that I had found a brother. Where conversations about tracing Mary and Orlando were short and consisted mainly of my updating them as to how the search was progressing (or not). This was different. They wanted to know about John, about his family and about him. They even wanted to meet him and in Christmas 1987 when Ben and I finally decided to get married, my mother asked John, not only to come to the wedding but also to accompany her, with my brother Adam. This was a real step forward. It showed that even though my parents found the idea of my finding my birth parents difficult, they were, by inviting John, stating, in their own way, that they now understood my need to know. I greatly appreciated this.

CHAPTER FIVE

SUCCESS

A week after my reunion with John I began writing letters again. Firstly to the German official to ask him why on earth he had not put John and I in touch. The letter back from this man was typical of the lack of understanding towards siblings separated through adoption. Although he was happy to hear that we had found each other, it was not his job to reunite people and advised that I take the matter up with the local Social Services.

Throughout this search, not only for John, but also for Mary and Orlando, I have found that the personal views of those officials who respond to my enquiries actually decide whether or not I will gain any information. The Law simply does not provide a mandate for adoptees to insist that they be provided with information. As for siblings, there is no law that states that brothers and sister have a right to information about each other. Thus you are at the mercy of various officials and their personal views.

Working within a system of vague rules means that I often received vague answers to my letters. I wrote to the passport office to enquire whether Mary had a British passport, and also to the National Insurance department. Both these offices had the facility to trace individuals and yet both times the reply was the same. A standard form with various possible answers and the relevant ones ticked. In my case the passport office had ticked the box, "No passport issued for this person within the last ten years" and the National Insurance Dept. had ticked the "no forwarding address available."

The National Insurance ran a scheme whereby they would forward a letter to an individual, on your behalf. The letter had to be sent open and if forwarded it was left to the individual to choose whether to reply or not. This appeared quite fair and allowed the person you were searching for to decide on what action to take. What is frustrating is that, as the enquirer, you are never told all the facts, just given a vague statement.

"No forwarding address" could mean that they once had an address and Mary may not be paying National Insurance. Or it could mean that she had left the country. No passport application could mean a number of things. There were never any direct answers to my questions.

I wrote next to the Norwegian Embassy in London. A few weeks later I was invited to meet the Norwegian Consul and asked to bring all my information. This meeting was very encouraging. The Consul spent some two hours going over all the information I had. He was sure that with the small population in Norway he would be able to find Mary's mother. It was an unusual Norwegian name. This gave me hope.

Whilst in London I went from the Embassy to Somerset House to see whether I could find any information about Mary's father, Archibald Brown. Somerset House has a wonderful system, far simpler than St Catherine's House. Instead of four volumes of books per year, there is just one book for each year that records all deaths with in that year. I had the year of Archibald's death and within a matter of an hour had found the entry for him.

It was just one page. It gave the date of his death and a copy of his Will in which he had left everything to his wife. Where Archibald's wife had signed the Will, she had also provided her address at the time of his death in 1943. This was a North London address. I knew it was most unlikely that my natural grandmother still lived at that address. It was some forty-five years old and I thought the most likely thing was that she had gone back to Norway.

What struck me as odd was that Mary was born in 1938 and from the dates on Archibald's Will was probably born here in England. Having paid for a copy of the Will I immediately went to St Catherine's House and quite quickly found Mary's entry of birth. She had, indeed, been born in Finchley, north London.

I was just becoming convinced that the Norwegian ancestry bit was probably false when the Consul telephoned me to say that he had found my natural grandmother.

Sitting in his office one week later the Consul was visibly so excited by his find he kept reverting back to his native Norwegian. Between the strange words I understood that he had found a woman by the same name as Mary's mother and that she was living in a nursing home just outside Oslo. He had telephoned the home and although they confirmed that she was there they also explained to him that she was senile and didn't even know her own name.

I wasn't sure whether to be happy at this find or not, but then the Consul said there was more, and from behind his desk produced a large book. On the front were the words (in Norwegian) "About the family N......" It appeared that Mary's family was well known within Norway and so had documented their own history. The Consul had copied all relevant pages to do with "my line" as he called it.

Immediately I realised that the woman residing in the home in Norway could not be the person I was looking for as in the ancestral book, my natural grandmother, Lucinda, was listed as being born on August 13th 1900, England, not Oslo. The proof came with a listing for her husband Archibald and their four children, one of which was Mary. The last entry stated the same address as on Archibald's Will. The entry was made in 1975 at the time the book was compiled.

I explained this to the Consul and he was delighted that he had played a part in my search. He told me that in Norway the government actually provides a service to help adoptees trace their natural families. The attitude towards searching was positive and this was shown in the time and effort this man gave me in order to help me find Mary's family.

I went home and wrote a letter to the Finchley address. A couple of weeks later I received a call. A lady said that she was sorry but she had opened my letter and felt that it was only fair to inform me that my natural grandmother had moved house several years ago. I didn't mind her opening the letter and I wasn't surprised by this news. I asked half-heartedly whether she might have a forwarding address for Lucinda and there was a long pause. Then with a chuckle she said, "Yes, I do. Your grandmother only moved next door."

"Next door?"

"Yes, she lives next door to me, but she is moving away in three weeks time and I do not know where she is going. I thought you would like to know."

This was certainly an understatement. The timing was incredible. The lady said she would try and pass on my number to the son who still lived with Lucinda. He apparently walked past her house each day and was "far more friendly than his mother".

I thanked the woman and waited for a call. It came the next day.

It seemed strange to be talking with my natural uncle. He said that his mother Lucinda would like to meet me and could I visit the following Saturday. I agreed. His voice, although friendly, sounded anxious; he did not ask any questions and as soon as I said I would come, he finished the call.

Ben and I arrived in North London ten minutes early and so sat in the car for a while. I was wondering whether I should let Lucinda know that I wasn't the only child Mary had. Maybe she already knew. There was the small worry in my mind about Mary. It was obvious from my uncle's call that Mary was not with them, but I wondered whether she was still alive. Maybe they were going to break some bad news; I had the feeling of wanting to stop right there and not go any further with this reunion.

This was it: I was about to meet my natural grandmother. I had never known my adopted grandparents. My parents being older than average meant that my grandparents had all died when I was quite young. This made me feel very unsure about the meeting.

Ben climbed out of the car and indicated that I should do the same. We had parked a little way away from the house, which allowed us to walk back along the neat tree-lined road where Mary had grown up. As we approached the Victorian semi-detached house, we could see a tiny figure of a lady waiting in the front garden. She was so small and thin I felt as though I could just blow her over with one breath. She was so wrinkly that I wasn't sure whether the expression on her face was good or bad; it was impossible to gauge what she thought. I saw Ben's eyebrows rise slightly and he gripped my hand tighter as if to say, "Be careful, she could drop dead of a heart attack at the slightest shock."

As we approached, her face wrinkled even more as she smiled and reached forward to give me a kiss. As she kissed me she said, "You are Mary's, you are the image of her." I had never thought that this could be possible and couldn't wait to see a picture of Mary. Lucinda then invited us inside. We followed behind her as she moved very slowly, slightly swaying and tottering. It was most alarming.

Inside the house most of the furnishings had been packed in readiness for the move. The house had obviously seen better days and Lucinda was anxious to describe the way it had looked in its prime. She kept apologising for the many boxes that had been assembled in chaotic piles in the hallway.

I couldn't believe my good fortune at having made contact with her before the event. I knew that if I had delayed writing to the old address by just three weeks, I probably would have never been able to trace her, as she had not given her future address to the neighbour.

We were shown into a sitting room and nearly tripped over a dog lead.

"Sorry but he has to stay tied up, he's so naughty," Lucinda said.

One end of the lead was attached to a table, the other to a small dog who on seeing us enter the room, bounced off a settee and immediately tried to attach itself to one of Ben's legs.

"Get down you silly beast," Lucinda yelled at the animal, which immediately returned to the settee. It sat on one side of the settee and we were invited to sit on the other.

Lucinda offered us a cup of tea, we tried to say no as, in her fragile state, we thought it would probably take the remainder of the afternoon for her to make it to the kitchen, but she insisted. We sat back and waited. Then, instead of tottering and swaying, she tiptoed back out of the sitting room, neatly jumping over the dog lead as she went. Within five minutes she returned, tray in hand. Ben jumped to his feet to help her with the tray, but the dog jumped and attached itself to Ben who had to concentrate on removing the creature from his thigh. Lucinda took no notice of this and proceeded, with the tray of cups, to leap over the lead and make it to a small coffee table.

Once the situation with the dog had calmed down, we were given our tea. My natural grandmother spent a long while just staring at me and then in a small, slightly shaky voice declared: "I never knew, you know. About you, I never knew…"

"Mary never told you?" I enquired

"I don't understand it," she continued. "Mary lived at home with me until 1979. How could she get pregnant without me knowing? I am your grandmother, I should have known. I would never have let her give you up…….never."

I remember apologising at this point. I'm not sure why, but someone needed to. I did wonder how Mary had managed to conceal her pregnancies from her own mother.

Lucinda then questioned me as to when I was born and how I had come to find her. She did not question anything I said, just repeated several times "I had no idea about you, really."

I asked if she had any pictures of Mary. Lucinda stood and collected some photograph albums. She opened one and handed it to me. The picture was of a woman in her early twenties, thick, curly black hair. Large blue eyes and a trim figure, she was holding a kitten close to her and smiling. "That's Mary." Lucinda said.

Apart from my colouring - I have mousy brown hair - there was a similarity in our faces. Ben immediately thought this and Lucinda kept on repeating, "There is no doubt she is your mother, you are so alike." Because I wanted to look like her, to feel that I had come from this woman, I found a likeness quite quickly. It was strange as all the times in my past when I had been convinced that some stranger was my natural mother, I had chosen someone with the same colouring and build as me. It is peculiar, but I expected to look like Mary's twin and of course this was not the case. Genetics become all jumbled up and each generation only inherits certain features. In this case, I could recognise my eyes and the long shape of my face as being almost identical to Mary's. Mary was, however, a good two inches taller than me and much darker in colouring than I had expected.

"Is Mary well?" I enquired. Lucinda moved slowly back to her seat and her voice became weak and shaky as she spoke about her daughter.

"She is not in this country," she began. "She left in 1979." I immediately noted that that was the year I turned eighteen and started searching.

"Why did she leave?" My question was not answered. Instead Lucinda looked at me and then asked if I knew who my father was. I said I had a name for him and told her the name. She did not know that person and then went into a long speech about how Mary had not known any men. She was a good girl, quiet and home loving. Where had she met him?

I said I didn't know, but that he was a married man who was thirty-seven years old at the time of my birth and had been hoping for a divorce.

Lucinda's face grew pale, and she was pale anyway, but it was as though she had seen a ghost. Ben looked visibly anxious but was unable to move towards her because the dog was waiting to pounce.

"My God, Him. No it couldn't be, Mary would not have..." Her voice trailed off. We waited in silence as Lucinda took some slow deep breaths and then continued. "There was only one man that I knew of, but he was a bad man, a dangerous man and you must not look for him. He is the reason Mary left the country. She had to get away from him. He tried to kill her."

Somehow this dramatic account seemed almost ridiculous and yet there was real fear in this old woman's eyes.

"It can't be him, though, as you are small and he was huge. Over six feet tall and broad. Very menacing. You are not like that; it can't be him."

I wondered if it would be prudent to explain about John at this point. Lucinda had in her last statement confirmed that this man, whoever he was, was our natural father.

Ben nudged me; he also thought now might be the right moment to tell her, and so I did. There is no easy way to tell someone this kind of news. Throughout the search I have found this aspect the most difficult. Most people can accept the possibility of one accidental pregnancy, but two! That brought with it the image of irresponsibility and so made unspoken judgements about a person's morality.

Lucinda did not react in a shocked way, but just kept saying. "But how? Two children. How did she manage to keep you both a secret? I would have known if she was pregnant, surely."

I described John's physical build to Lucinda who then realised that the man both she and Mary had feared was most likely to be our birth father.

"He showed us divorce papers, you know," she continued. "Brought them around and sat right here with me, as you are now. Good looking, he was, but it was all untrue. He never got a divorce. I warned Mary to stay away from him and I thought she had. Stupid girl, now I understand."

Lucinda's voice had gathered strength; it was as though she had forgotten she was meant to be a frail old lady.

"I can't tell you where Mary is…I'm not allowed," she declared.

The tone in her voice was now firm, almost scolding. "No," she went on. "Mary has suffered enough. She is very unwell, you know."

"No, I didn't know," I quickly jumped in. "What is wrong with her?"

"When she left England, she had cancer of the thyroid gland. It has been removed but she is not well. He got her a job, you know." Lucinda became calm again. "Got her sacked from Foyle's book shop and then found her a new job. A very important job as a secretary in an office in London. She worked very well there, was thought of highly. Both your Uncle Andy and I worked for her too." She stood again and went over to a drawer, opened it and pulled out a piece of white paper on which was stuck a newspaper cutting. It was dated 1962 and was an article about a South African dissident.

"Andy and I would spend hours cutting out these articles for Mary. Each paper had to be read and then anything written on South Africa had to be cut out, dated and stuck on to a sheet of A4 paper. Andy would travel to London once a week to hand them in."

None of this made sense to me but she continued, "He did not like what Mary was doing; started making life difficult for her, Mary told him to go but he wouldn't. Kept saying he would kill her and so after being knocked down by a van in 1979, she left the country."

At this point the door opened and in walked a man. He was small, around five feet, five with the longest beard I had ever seen. He reminded me of a troll, but I needed no introduction: this was Andy, Mary's younger brother and my natural uncle.

By now Ben was deciding whether it would be best to break off his engagement to me. It was obvious that my natural family consisted of some very strange characters and there was a growing possibility that madness may run in this family. I found Uncle Andy's appearance almost comical. It was as though we had stepped through the wardrobe into the land of Narnia and were now in the presence of the White Witch and her Troll.

Andy did not say anything to us. A faint smell of alcohol followed him over to a large armchair where he sat and proceeded to fill and light a pipe. Every so often he would glance at me. His eyes were incredible. Huge and green, extraordinarily beautiful and yet almost hidden by a mass of black hair.

"Well, there is no doubt who you are," he declared. He was, like his mother, well spoken, but his voice was quiet. "It is like being in the room with Mary."

At this point Lucinda stood and proceeded to tiptoe out of the room, again jumping over the dog lead. The dog suddenly noticed that Andy was in the room and leapt towards him where he was greeted with much fuss. Ben excused himself and went to find a loo. This left Andy, the dog and myself alone.

"She's in New Zealand." Andy started "Did Ma give you her address?"

I explained what had happened and Andy did not comment.

The door swung open and Lucinda came back in. "Tea time. Please sit around the table." Lucinda pointed to a semi-circular table that stuck out from a wall in the sitting room. I obeyed and was shown a seat. When Ben returned he was shown to another and then Andy sat. Lucinda brought in the tea.

I have been brought up to be polite and eat what you are given, especially at someone else's house. So has Ben. There was only one item of food on the plate. It had obviously been prepared earlier and, by the state of its decomposition, some days earlier.

"Get stuck in, please. Don't wait for me. I'm not eating," Lucinda declared. The enthusiasm in her voice indicated that it had taken considerable effort to prepare this meal.

A piece of tongue sat in front of each of us, dried out and turning rather green. I did not dare look at Ben but could make out that Andy had almost finished his. So there was no choice; we ate it! Lucinda was thrilled and offered us more. We managed to decline by making various excuses and then we waited whilst she prepared and ate her own tea. It consisted of a milky fluid meal that she sucked up on a spoon.

Andy took no notice of the slurping sounds and proceeded to eat more pieces of tongue. I began to wonder what life would have been like to grow up in this house. There was something about Lucinda that just did not seem right. She presented herself as an extremely frail old lady and yet there was a twinkle in her eye that showed she was not missing a word or expression.

From time to time she had become quite involved with the conversation and then the frailty had vanished, exchanged instead for a confident, quite firm manner and voice. One thing she was consistent about, however, was that I should, under no circumstances, try and find my natural father as he could hurt me.

Each time Lucinda spoke about him she spoke, it seemed, in riddles. Words like dangerous and bad were frequently used. When she saw that I was not reacting to these descriptions with any appropriate concern, she moved closer towards me and in a tiny squeaky desperate voice she whispered, "He was a spy, you know."

I longed to ask questions: the word spy was said with such fear that it was almost comical and I did not dare speak for fear of laughing.

Lucinda had talked about Mary's work as though this had some direct connection to my natural father and when I asked her to explain the exact nature of Mary's work, she would not, but just repeated over and over that I should not, under any circumstances, try and find Orlando.

Of course, if there was one thing that would spur my curiosity on it was being told not to do something. Each time Lucinda told me not to start searching for Orlando I instantly wanted to do exactly that. Not because she had said not to, but because she would not give any tangible reasons for declaring that this man was "dangerous". I could not understand how my birth mother would have two children by a man who then proceeded, as Lucinda claimed, to try and kill her. It did not make sense, but definitely activated my imagination.

We stayed with Lucinda and Andy until around 6pm. On leaving I asked if she would be willing to forward a letter from me to Mary. This way she would not have to give me any information about Mary's whereabouts and Mary could have the choice of whether or not to contact me. Lucinda said she would think about it.

Andy did not say goodbye. Full of rotten tongue, he had fallen asleep in an armchair, the dog curled up on top of him. Ben was not slow to leave the house. As we rounded the corner away from Lucinda's view, Ben looked at me. "They are all bonkers. You should be grateful you did not grow up there."

He was right, of course. A second reality dawned. The rosy picture I had of a natural family did not contain the possibility that they would all be "bonkers".

"I'm not going there again," Ben stated. "Fran, have you thought about what Mary might be like?"

I hadn't, and at this point did not really want to. Ben did not go back again, but I did. Shortly after our visit, Lucinda called and said she wanted to meet John. Would we like to come for tea? We went, (not for tea), but we went.

John's physical size immediately brought a different reaction. She did not play the senile old thing again. Instead she was completely in control and quite adamant that we should understand how dangerous it was for us to continue our search.

Andy sat silent the whole time. The dog made a valiant attempt to abuse John, but got a quick and instant scolding which allowed John to move quite freely around the room whilst the animal resorted instead to trying to mate with several cushions on a settee.

It seemed to alarm both Lucinda and Andy that John wanted to join the police force. They were openly worried about this.

John is polite and friendly but does not tolerate "vagueness". Direct answers to direct questions is the way he deals with people and so Lucinda was not given the chance to play at being senile.

It was, in fact, a far better visit. Lucinda told us that Mary now lived in New Zealand and she agreed to send a letter I had brought with me.

We did not have to suffer tea and left after a pleasant visit. John was not, however, impressed with the thought of his genetic inheritance.

We both knew that the only way we could solve the mystery about Orlando and Mary would be to find them. My letter was now on its way to New Zealand and so I felt that it was only going to be a short time before all was revealed.

Mary, however, did not reply to me immediately. The day my letter arrived on her doorstep in Auckland, the uncle with whom she lived, died. I was to wait nearly a year before receiving a reply.

It was now ten years since I had posted my application for my original birth certificate. I was now adult and married. Ben and I wanted children and we were on the waiting list for IVF treatment. My adopted parents, still not happy at my strong desire to know my past, had been given ten years to get used to the idea. I think they thought I would probably never find my birth parents. From time to time I shared this thought. There would be months when I would get on with my life quite happily and not give much thought to whether or not Mary would ever write to me and then there were days when I longed to know why she had not replied straight away. I knew that she had received my letter as Lucinda had let me know this, but the waiting during this year was terrible.

CHAPTER SIX

ROLAND

On a bright crisp morning in autumn 1988 a letter finally arrived from New Zealand. It was now ten months since I had left my letter with Lucinda to forward to Mary. I opened the letter and recognised, from my Social Service records, the still child-like handwriting of my birth mother. Contact was finally made.

Mary's letter was filled with the grief she was suffering at the loss of her uncle. She described their life together as idyllic and the only happiness she had ever experienced. She also talked at length about her "babies". Not John and I, but her five cats and her beloved dog, Henry. The letter was written as though to a small child, telling of the "naughty things" her "little ones" got up to and how much she loved them. It was a sad letter. I was not expecting this. Mary appeared to be so innocent, so caught up in a world of soft warm fluffy animals.

I had so many questions that I wanted to ask her, it was tempting just to scribble them all down in a letter and demand answers, but from her reply to my first letter I already felt more as a parent to Mary. It was also very obvious that the grief she was going through was causing her ill health and an inability to deal with any personal questions.

With her letter came another from a lady named Helen. Helen, a Macmillan nurse had looked after Mary's uncle during his last few months of life. After the uncle had died, Helen had become concerned about Mary's mental health and had formed a friendship with her. Now Mary had confided in her about my existence and Helen wanted to let me know that Mary was unwell. Unwell because she was an agoraphobic and an alcoholic.

Helen's letter painted my first picture of Mary. It told how Mary had suffered at the hands of my birth father and only found happiness when she joined her uncle. They had spent seven years together before his death from lung cancer. During those seven years they had virtually lost all contact with the outside world and only existed for each other and the various animals they kept.

Helen's letter also warned me that I was to have no contact with my birth father "Roland". I was confused. Suddenly his name was not Orlando, but Roland. It was strange but I remember thinking some time earlier that the name Orlando was so peculiar it could be an anagram of Roland.

I wanted to reply to Mary's letter but knowing that I would not be able to ask anything of any importance found it very difficult. I chose instead to send her some pictures of my wedding. The pictures also included John. A reply came almost by return. She was thrilled to see what I looked like. This sparked her ability to write a little more as she commented that John was the splitting image of his birth father. As if caught in a moment of reminiscence, she disclosed Roland's old address from the time she knew him.

There was now a new emotion showing in her words. Anger. Mary scrawled pages about Roland and how he threatened her and manipulated her life. Then as though remembering that she should not speak about him, her writing changed direction and the subject matter reverts to the cats.

I knew at this point that the mother I had originally been searching for, the one that would understand me was not there, and never had been. If I had, at eighteen years old been reunited with Mary, it would have been a complete disaster as I would not have found a mother and certainly would not have been equipped to cope with her next disclosure. My fantasies of being a "love" child and the romantic picture I relied on to get me through several years of unhappiness were shattered in an instant when she explained in her letter that I was, in fact, conceived because Roland had raped her.

This letter took much time to come to terms with. I had never considered being the product of a rape. This changed everything and made me wonder how she felt about me contacting her. There was also the small problem of John. Was he the product of rape too? And if so, how was it that she stayed in contact with Roland after my birth only to get raped again.

I knew at this stage that I needed to find my birth father. I was sure that just by seeing him I would know what the truth was but Mary, Helen, Lucinda and Andy had all given such dramatic accounts of this man that I was not sure of how to approach this search.

During 1988 did not search for Roland. I spent this year concentrating on establishing Mary's trust. Letters moved back and forth from New Zealand. I wrote about the weather, our two cats, Ben and my desire to have children, my work and basically anything that I knew would not threaten her. In return she wrote about her garden, her cats and dog and housework. It was, although wonderful to have contact with her, also completely frustrating because of the lack of information and limits to our conversations.

However as the months progressed I found that each of her letters contained just one little piece of information about her past life and so I began to separate those clues from the rest of her writing and slowly a picture emerged.

It was of a lonely young girl, swept off her feet by an older man. He was charming and protective of her. He finds her work and supports her emotionally. Once she has completely fallen in love with him, he rapes her and she becomes pregnant. At this point she finds out he is already married. He promises to get a divorce but this never happens. She is now working for him and he is continuing to "force himself" upon her. She becomes pregnant again. She tries to leave him but he begins to threaten her, saying that he will have her babies killed if she ever leaves him. She is trapped. Once trapped he then gets her to hand information to him from her work. He sells the information she gives.

The truth surrounding Mary and Roland was becoming more complicated than a John Le Carre novel. Ben and I spent many hours discussing the possibilities of what actually happened between them. There seemed so much confusion and coupled with Mary's obvious drinking problem, the writing was often inconsistent and muddled.

In May 1989 I was still working for the Social Services. A call came through to the office early on a Tuesday morning. My sister Amy had died. Her death was not expected although she had been ill for several months with persistent bouts of pneumonia. It was May 2nd. My mother's birthday.

Ben and I immediately travelled to my adopted parent's house in London. My mother and father had been to see Amy. It had not been a peaceful death; it appeared that because she was unable to say she was in pain, no attempt had been made to administer pain relief.

Amy's whole life was as a never-ending grief for my parents. The only comfort they found in her death was that they had outlived her. Their fear was as so many parents of profoundly handicapped people that if they died, there would be no one left to care. It was a strange day. The tears were really for a person who had been denied a life. Given only seven years to live she had gone on to survive for a further twenty-five. There was a feeling that now, only now after thirty-three years they could finally mourn for the daughter they had lost.

The funeral was terrible. There was hardly anyone there. Just the hospital staff, patients from Amy's ward and a few relatives. As adopted children were placed in secrecy; children who were not born "perfect" were also hushed away. The stigma of illegitimacy and the stigma of having a handicapped child went hand in hand. To be able to say, "It's over" as my mother did several times that day, meant, for her that she no longer had to keep her own "little secret" hidden. Amy's death brought release, not only from the pain Amy was suffering but also from the pain of always wondering what memories and events my parents would have shared with her if she had not been so terribly damaged.

A birth mother who is separated from her baby at birth is also thrown into a life-long world of grief where the "I wonder what he/she is doing now…" occupies the mind. It is by all accounts a very similar grief. But, where as a birth mother who never has any contact with her offspring can always hope and dream; my parents faced the reality of their situation each time they visited their daughter and this was a weekly reminder of "what might have been?" if things had been different.

Following Amy's death I decided not to waste time waiting for Mary to tell me the truth. I decided to write a letter to the address Mary had given for Roland in her first letter to me. It was now late 1989 and I was expecting our first child. Ben's predictions had been correct and although we had started IVF treatment, this baby had been conceived naturally, much to our delight and much to the disbelief of my doctor, who thought I was having a pseudo-pregnancy and wanted me to see a psychiatrist. It took three pregnancy tests to convince him otherwise.

By this stage I realised that all my original reasons for searching were changing yet again. Expecting a baby brought with it new questions. I was about to bring a new life into the world I wanted to know my past, not only for me but also for the baby.

In December 1989 I received a telephone call. It was from a woman and she did not sound friendly.
"Is this a paternity suit?" She asked. "Why are you trying to contact Roland?"
" Who are you?" I asked
"I'm his wife" She replied. "Who are you?"
I didn't know what to say. The woman's voice was so aggressive in its tone. It was hard, very business like, as though she had taken calls like this before and was routinely going through one of them again.
I told her that I was working on behalf of a young man who was trying to trace his birth father. I told her that Roland was the birth father's name.
She did not try and deny it, instead said that I could not speak with Roland as he was in hospital. She would tell him when he returned home.

About two weeks later my birth father telephoned. His voice was firm but gentle. He did not have the German accent I expected, but a soft Lancashire accent, very similar to John's. He did not ask me who I worked for or how I got his old address, just said he wished to meet John. We arranged the meeting on John's birthday, 7th March. My birth father said we were to meet him in the café at the Royal festival Hall.

To be honest, whilst speaking with him I wanted to tell him who I was, but being pregnant and having been told that so many negative things about him I decided it would be safer to just remain in the role of intermediary. This provided me with the best chance of getting away from a situation if I needed too.

John and I met at Waterloo Station. I was six months pregnant, but looked almost ready to give birth. It dawned on me that as Lucinda thought I looked like Mary then Roland might recognise me. Also I may remind him more of Mary because I was pregnant. My head was filled with the stories I had heard about him. How he was a spy. How he had killed people and was dangerous. How he had "forced himself" on my birth mother. I thought of the descriptions I had of him being over six-foot tall, with fair hair and blue eyes. How his collar measurement was 18 inches and that you couldn't fail to spot him in a crowd as he had a "particular" walk, strong and upright, quite impressive.

I had a picture of a huge man with a loud booming voice and a firm manner. Someone you did not argue with, someone you treated with care. I wasn't sure how I felt about this but I did feel excited by the element of mystery and danger. It made me think of spy novels and great adventures; the only difference was that we were about to meet the "baddie" and this small fact kept my imagination in check.

We arrived at the Festival Hall an hour early. John wanted to "check it out" first and to make sure that the meeting place was appropriate and safe. The fact that the building was busy provided a sense of security. The silly thing was that neither of us knew why, exactly, we were worried. Roland need not have made any contact. There was no way I could have found out where he was living now as my original enquiry had been passed on to his wife. John was doing his "police" thing. Checking the cars parked close by, jotting down the number plates so that we could maybe find Roland's address from one of them at a later stage.

My adopted brother, Adam, who worked in London at the time, had also come to the Festival Hall. He had been worried for me and offered to come and sit at another table, just in case! I think it was the "just in case" that I was reacting to most. Ten minutes before our meeting I disappeared into the Ladies toilet to tidy myself and practise calm expressions.

John bought some drinks and sat down. When I finally managed to exit the loo I looked across at the whole café area. There were about ten fixed tables and then a few others scattered around. There were only three people sitting, one was Adam and one, John. Right at the back there was a man sat facing everyone that entered the café. He was a large man, with grey-white hair. I felt convinced that this was Roland. Suddenly I wanted to laugh. It was all so ridiculous. All three of us were acting as though on some highly important covert operation. There was Adam, pretending to be engrossed in a Civil Engineering Magazine whilst every so often, catching my eye and giving me an "I'm ready for anything" wink. John, on the other hand, not looking around at all, instead leaning right back in a chair, he was pretending to be absorbed in a menu whilst slowly blowing out long streams of tobacco smoke from what appeared to be an endless cigarette. Then there was me. Six months pregnant, with no bladder control and wearing a dress that resembled a large green tent, trying to look sophisticated, as though I was enjoying a cultural day out in London.

I joined John and sat with my back facing the man. Adam sat some tables behind. I was so sure that the man on the last table was Roland I was waiting for his approach. Instead from in front of me a man appeared. He said nothing but indicated that he was going to sit beside me. I shuffled up and he sat down next to me and opposite John.
The first thing I noticed was that he had dark hair, almost black. It was heavy greased and swept back off his face. Far from appearing

huge, he looked of average height and a slim build. He was dressed completely in brown. A neat brown jacket with a waist tie and brown trousers. He carried nothing.

"You must be John," he said in a quiet voice. The two men shook hands. I noticed how large Roland's hands were. As they shook hands he smiled at John. It was a kind smile, hardly that of a killer, although I have not met many murderers or rapists and so found it very difficult to know what exactly I was looking for. The total difference in his appearance made me instantly wonder if this was really our birth father. If he were so dangerous and wanting to keep his identity a secret it would have been easy to send someone in his place. We would not know.

I decided the only way of determining who he was, was to tell him my original name. This man was, quite obviously not dangerous. If this were the real Roland, then I would know, by his reaction. If it wasn't then it wouldn't matter, so I told him who I was.

His reaction was unexpected. I do not know what I thought he would say or do, but I did not expect to see his eyes fill with tears. He just starred at me. He did not say anything but for a few minutes he was quite overcome and had to calm himself. Once composed he asked me when the baby was due?

"June," I replied. He nodded and smiled and then offered us both a drink.

We spent three hours with Roland. During that time he talked about himself and his life. He spoke so quietly that it was, at times almost impossible to hear what he was saying. We walked along the Thames together and he insisted on buying us both lunch. Throughout the whole time he did not eat or drink anything.

Just before we parted he reached into his jacket pocket and pulled out an envelope bound with several elastic bands. Carefully he removed the elastic bands and opened the envelope. Inside was another little packet from which he removed a photograph. It was of Mary and him together, on a boat. They are sitting and smiling towards the camera and he had his arm around her. It made me want to know who had taken the picture as there was something quite intimate about it as though they had known the third person, as though it was a family holiday snap. He said it was taken in Berlin in the early 60's and of course I did not ask any questions, just thanked him for the picture.

John had hoped to catch a glimpse of the car Roland had brought with him to our meeting. Roland insisted instead on escorting us both back to Waterloo station. My train left first and Roland stood with me until it was time for it to leave. As the train pulled away I could see him escorting John to the underground. I saw them shake hands, and then they were out of sight.

His last words to me were, "There is much more to Mary than you will ever know." What he meant by this I did not know, but it implied the same mystery and danger that had surrounded him. In the time we had shared together he had managed to actually say nothing of any importance. The only thing he had asked about Mary was whether we were in contact with her. For her safety I had said that we made contact but there was now none. Both John and I felt it would be better not to let either of them think that we were in contact with the other. Mary would most definitely "hit" the drink if she knew and most probably never trust me again. Roland did not need to know anything about Mary's life now.

I was pleased to have met my birth father. I was also relieved that I had told him who I was. This was, however, the only meeting I would ever have with him.

On May 3rd I gave birth to a son. This was just one year and a day after my sister Amy's death. I had a strong feeling that this baby would come early. Six weeks early and weighing only four and a half pounds he raced into the world in less than two hours. We named him Tobias. It would be romantic to say that he was called this after Tobias and the Angel, but his name came out of the fact that I always referred to my pregnancy as "To be or not to be? This became Toby and just to give him a more formal option, Tobias.

Toby was not the most beautiful baby at birth. Being so premature meant that he did not fit his skin. He resembled the cartoon character Mr Magoo. I have never found newborn babies beautiful and although the team of doctors and midwives all congratulated me on the birth of a beautiful baby boy, I was not convinced. Ben was with me during the birth and first to hold our son. Then Toby was whisked away from us and placed in the Special Care Unit.

I was placed on a ward with two other new mums. Both of these ladies had babies in Special Care and so there were no babies to be seen. As I sat there I found it impossible to sleep or simply wait for news about my baby and, so made my way to the Special Care unit and insisted that I be allowed to stay with him. I remember starring at this infant and knowing that I could not have done what Mary did. It did not matter how small or scrawny this baby was, he was part of me and I could never part with him. The instant bond between mother and baby was there. I wondered how any woman could bear to part with her own child.

Now as a mother, I could feel the guilt and shame that birth mothers must experience when they give up a baby. Just thinking about parting with this little scrap of a baby brought instant tears. Mother Nature intends us to be good parents. A baby can be as ugly as sin or completely different in looks or nature to how we imagined. It does not matter, as every parent will automatically think his or her baby is the most wonderful child in the world. This is, I think, nature's way of protecting that offspring, of making sure that it is loved and nurtured to maturity. To give up a baby conflicts with the deepest instincts within us as human beings.

Believing also that you will never see your baby again and yet never knowing where he or she has gone must be unbearable. The fear of birth mothers is centred on shame and guilt. They have had to defy Mother Nature itself in order to give away their own offspring and then after years of coping or not coping with their "secret", the baby, now a full grown adult can turn up wanting to know why they did it.

Suddenly I understood why Mary was so reluctant for me to find her. I had only ever thought of this search from my own needs, but from a birth mother's point of view, there was always a possibility that a child might be seeking revenge for being abandoned. In Mary's case there were the added "scandals". She was unmarried, having a relationship with a married man and had become pregnant twice. It now made sense that she chose to believe that both John and I were the product of two rapes.

Becoming a mother also brought with it a new respect for my adopted parents. They had also done something I now knew I could never do. Adopt. Every time I held Toby or fed him I knew I could not love someone else's child as much as my own. I could never adopt. This was a shameful realisation for me.

Before having Toby, Ben and I did consider adoption. If we had been unable to have any children of our own we may have chosen this route. An adopted child placed with a childless couple never has to compete with the couple's natural offspring for love. They are equal within the family unit. It would be almost impossible to feel and give the same "unconditional" love to both a child of your own and an adopted child. It would be natural to bond more deeply with your own child.

CHAPTER SEVEN

HOME TRUTHS

During the hot summer of 1990 my time was fully occupied with the care of our newborn son. Not only was he my first experience of caring for a baby, but being premature and small, feeding was time-consuming and difficult. He also did not seem to require much sleep. Ben had just been employed as a Publisher within the Aerospace Industry and his job frequently took him abroad.

This was a difficult time for me, as I had no help. I could go for days without having a conversation with another adult. We had moved, during the pregnancy from our tiny house in Windsor to a three-bedroom semi –detached house in near-by Egham and because Toby had arrived early I had missed nearly all the antenatal meetings with other expectant mums. This was a time that I felt I really needed a "mum" to help and support me. My adopted mum lived in London and was now in her mid-seventies. Although she wanted to help, her life was still enormously active with interests of her own and the distance between us made it impossible to just pop around.

Mary, my birth mother, not only lived on the other side of the world but even if she had lived close by, she would not have been sober enough to help and as far as I could tell, may well have not wanted to get involved. There seemed a strange irony that I had twice the normal amount of mothers and yet was totally unable to share the problems of motherhood with either of them.
Ben's mother and father helped when they could but having adopted a baby whilst on their last tour in Fiji, they were now, in their early sixties and fully occupied with the daily activities of an energetic six year old.
I did manage to meet a group of new mums and once a week we met up to share mutual "horror" stories and discuss our babies. It was not enough though and having spent twenty-four hours of each day

trying to calm an agitated and sleepless baby was making feel as though my brain was turning into rapidly into a sponge.

Isolation brought with it guilt of its own. I had wanted a baby for so long and now he was here I found I resented the total dependency he had on me. Wanting to be a good mother and not wanting in anyway repeat history by neglecting him or giving him to someone else to bring up meant that I felt I had to be with him all the time.

Motherhood, I found, not only difficult because I was constantly tired but also incredibly frightening. I was responsible for this infant and wanted to show that I could cope. This meant that when relatives did visit I would not tell them of the problems and worries I had but tried to give a picture of a well-organised, almost perfect mother.

I had been brought up in the care of au-pair girls. Most of them were barely adults themselves and few spoke English. I felt strongly that it was vital that I was the one who brought Toby up, partly because I was adopted and partly because I simply did not trust the idea of childminders bringing up my child. What I had not realised was that if you spend twenty-four hours of each and every day with a baby you become utterly boring to be with. You also lose your identity as an individual.

Then something happened to jolt me out of my growing depression. Roland telephoned me. It was a Thursday afternoon in July. His voice was so welcome to me as Ben was away and yet again there was no one to talk with. I remember that I just started to pour out my woes to him about motherhood and he listened. It was great. He asked about "baby" things and we had a long discussion about nappies. Quite bizarre really. Then he said he was pleased to be a grandfather again. I had not consciously made this connection between him and Toby; Roland was indeed another grandfather. I asked if he would like to meet me again but he said that he was unable to "get away". He talked about his wife as though she ruled his every move and explained that he would only be able to call when she was out.

Then he asked whether I had heard from Mary. I had agreed with John that it was best not to pass any information between the two and so said I hadn't. He paused and then changed the subject and asked me what hobbies I had.

I remember wishing at that moment that my life was filled with interesting things to say but apart from being a mum I simply had no time to pursue my interest in writing. Roland then told me how he liked to write and we discussed the type of stories that interested us. He said that he had written a book and it had been published. I was impressed and yet he would not tell me what the book was about only that he now wanted to write ghost stories.

We must have spoken for an hour. It was great and much easier to hear him over the telephone, than when I had been with him. He asked if he could call me again and I said that I would look forward to it. After his call I realised that I still did not have an address for him or a phone Number. I decided this did not matter, as he knew where I was and with the problems that he had it was probably best to leave the contact to him.

So began a year when I was regularly in contact with both Mary and Roland. Neither of them knew about the contact I had with the other and the stories they disclosed to me completely conflicted.

Mary's drinking was beginning to take its toll. The facts surrounding her past and of her life with Roland were becoming more dramatic. What was also emerging was that Mary had been both emotionally and physically abused by her mother Lucinda and a man who lived in the family home after her father Archibald's death. Through her account of her life she had been used and abused by all those she had been close to. Apart from her uncle who was pictured as a "knight in shining armour". Mary was convinced that Roland was still looking for her and that he was, as she often stated, "coming after her."

I was unable to tell her that this simply was not the case and that I was speaking with him regularly. I could not believe that his only reason for phoning me was to get to Mary, as he did not know I was in contact with her. I liked the man who called me. He was witty, softly spoken and able to share a conversation about anything from breast-feeding, to how he was trying to build a house for his disabled son.

The conversations we had were interesting and I dearly wanted to meet him again. This unfortunately was not to happen as he always had some reason for not being able to meet. He always said he would love to meet again, but that it was" impossible." Occasionally while we talked he would suddenly change the subject and begin to warn me to "be careful." Anyone could be listening to our calls or be watching me." I found these remarks absurd and always told him that I felt sorry for anyone who chose to watch me as my life was so utterly boring.

Roland's tone of voice during these short bursts of whispered warnings always changed. It was as though he were playing a game with me, trying to gauge my reaction to things.

I did not want to play this game. I found the notion that he and Mary were spies and that their lives were built on intrigue quite ridiculous. Something had obviously happened; they had planned or carried out some awful deed that involved personal risk, but what it was? I did not know and it did not matter how many questions I asked of both of them, their answers were confusing, like missing parts in a huge jigsaw puzzle.

In spring 1991 Ben and I lost a baby, another boy, stillborn at seven months. I was only just getting to grips with being a mum when I had found myself pregnant again. Toby was only seven months old and this new pregnancy was a total shock. The baby was due in August, but right from the start there had been problems. The first was that I was carrying twins: one was lost very early. This undoubtedly weakened the remaining pregnancy. The loss of this baby, we called David had a huge impact because I had not been pleased to learn that I was pregnant again and so felt tremendously guilty when the baby was lost.

Toby was only one year old and still not requiring much sleep. I was tired and cross at always being alone and Ben was trying hard to move up the career ladder. The strain was showing in us both.

In Autumn.1992 I received a letter from Helen. Mary was ill, gravely ill. Could I go out to New Zealand to meet her?

Although I had always wanted to meet by birth mother the opportunity had not arisen before. Firstly Mary had not, until then trusted me enough to contemplate a physical reunion and secondly my life was such that I simply did not have the child-care available in order to go to New Zealand alone.

Ben managed to re-arrange a business trip and my adopted father offered to lend me the money for the flight. There was a huge feeling from all the family that it would be a good idea, for several reasons if I went away for a while. If nothing else I would get a chance to rest and get some sleep.

It was strange as everyone viewed my forthcoming trip as a "needed" holiday. The reason for my going was never mentioned. The only person, who seemed to view this journey for what it really was, was John. I asked John whether he wanted to join me but found that far from wanting to meet his birth mother, he most definitely did not. John and I had shared all information about our birth parents and I knew that he had written to Mary, but John wanted answers and had no intention of playing games with her. He couldn't understand why I should wish to fly 14,000 miles to meet an alcoholic, agoraphobic with psychotic tendencies?

It was not until I was in the departure lounge at Heathrow. Bags packed and labelled. Toby and Ben safely housed with Ben's parents, and nothing to do but watch the hundreds of other travellers, that I began to think about what I was doing and wondered whether John was right. Helen had certainly painted a grim picture of Mary's mental health. What if Mary changed her mind and did not wish to meet me? What if, on seeing her I hated her? It was certainly a long way to go to make a mistake.

My flight was called.
Flight number one to San Francisco was fine. An exciting new experience. I felt tremendous freedom at being on my own with no responsibilities. Flight two to Honolulu was a little anxious as the man in the seat next to me died and I was given a "jump" seat to sit on whilst the crew rushed around keeping people calm and trying to ignore the frequent bouts of violent turbulence.

Due to the incident on the plane the next flight number three, to Auckland was delayed. I spent six idyllic hours sitting in an outside airport lounge at Honolulu, lapping up the evening sun. The smell of Frangipani and the deep colours of Hibiscus plants were wonderful. From the airport I could see a long road that led away up to a mountain. I had a strong desire just to grab my bags and follow that track.

The last part of this two-day journey was made on a DC10. The plane was packed but being a night flight everyone seemed to settle down very quickly. I had not slept since leaving London. I just did not want to miss any part of this adventure but now I was tired and although I wanted to keep awake, fell asleep almost straight away.

A shaft of light ran horizontally across the pitch-black sky. I woke to see the dawn emerge and the rising sun divide night from day. Its radiance brought a great sense of peace and destiny. There was only one hour to go before we landed in Auckland. Today, after a separation of thirty years, I would finally meet my birth mother.

Approaching Auckland airport the view from the aeroplane was of lush green fields, with sheep grazing. It looked so British and seemed peculiar that this country was so far away. Then a sign that I had not imagined this journey. A palm tree rising out of a field. This definitely was not England.

Helen met me at the airport. She came running towards me, a shoulder bag over her arm swinging frantically and her short, wavy hair bouncing over her eyes. She flung her arms round me, crying with excitement and babbling "welcomes" through the tears. Insisting on carrying my entire luggage, and then hurling the suitcase into the boot of her car and off we drove through the city of Auckland.
"Land of the Long White Cloud," Helen shouted above the noise of her car engine. "That's what the first settlers called this country." I looked out across a Peninsula to see the volcano *Wangaparoa*, rising out from the water.

"It's the same shape from where ever you view it," she added. Then she took one hand off the steering wheel, lowered her sunglasses and patted me on the arm. "Frannie, I'm so glad you are here."

We drove out of Auckland and into the suburbs. It was November 6th 1992; I had left behind a wet, grey and cold England to arrive in New Zealand during the spring. The sun was warm and spring flowers filled Helen's garden.

Her house was built on two levels. The ground floor housed a garage, a utility, a study and Helen and her husband Jim's bedroom. Upstairs there was the main area that included a kitchen and an enormous sitting/ dining area and two spare bedrooms. Helen showed me to the bedroom she had prepared for me. As she opened the door the scent of flowers filled the air as around the room several vases of flowers had been arranged as a welcome for me from Mary.

A card lay, unopened on a bedside table. Helen said I was to open it. It was from Mary. It read: to my little 5lb-baby girl, a welcome from your mother. I found these words and flowers very upsetting. Part of me had longed for this moment for a very long time but another part of me found that I was wishing that I had just stayed with my own little baby. Helen realised that jet lag was taking effect and so ordered me to have a shower whilst she went to collect Mary. I did not argue.

One hour later I stood face to face with my natural mother. Helen was beside herself with tears and laughter, her short but strong frame almost jumping up and down with excitement. Mary and I just stood, staring at each other as though a vague memory of each other was being re-born.

Mary stood upright and tall, about five foot eight inches. Her hair was black, long and very wavy. Her eyes, large and blue showed me instantly that she shared with me the same fear and uncertainty. She was wearing a long blue dress over which she wore a pure white cotton pinafore, trimmed with lace. Apart from the fact that she was in her mid-fifties, she resembled a frightened child. In her arms she carried a large white Bichon frise, onto which was attached a red, white and blue rosette.

Something inside me thought that I did remember this person. It was so strange but I recognised the smile that nervously greeted me. It felt good. It felt extraordinary. It was a huge relief, as though greeting a long-lost friend. I did not know whether to laugh or cry. I do not think that anyone was able to speak. When we did we all started at the same time and immediately burst out laughing. Within a few minutes the laughing had become crying. Tears that were completely uncontrollable and I felt the strong natural bond that existed between us, but had been forgotten for so many years.

Later that day we made a short journey through the suburbs of Auckland to Mary's home. A small white picket fence led the way into a rose-scented front garden. In the centre a white lilac tree, its branches heavily laden with sweet-smelling flowers. Ahead some steps that led up to a glass-panelled front door.

Mary's house was almost entirely glass fronted. Soft white lace curtains hung from each window, gathered to the sides with pink ribbons. From the middle of each window, more nets, cascading downwards and gathered together like sails on a tall ship. It was a curious sight, reminded me of a Doll's House. It was impossible for me to believe that behind this quaint exterior lived a woman who had been mixed up in espionage and danger.

Once inside it was as if in a toyshop. On every ledge, shelf, mantelpiece and tabletop stood bears. Soft brown teddy bears. Some small, some large, but all perfect. Each piece of furniture was buried in large laced cushions and around the room several small pictures of her uncle. The pictures were arranged with a candle on each side, like miniature shrines.

Mary took me by the hand and led me to the room she wished me to have if I stayed with her. The room was decorated in Beatrice Potter wallpaper. In front of me stood an elaborate brass bed covered in an embroidered pure white bedspread. In one corner of the room a toy pram with a baby doll. On a chest of drawers a bear, all dressed in pink and carrying a parasol. On the windowsill, tiny flower fairy statues .It was a fairy tale room for the fairy-tale child that Mary wanted to be. She had used this room when her uncle was alive but now she had prepared it for me.

The room made me feel sick. I found it macabre and wanted to run out of the house and away as fast as possible. I did not know how to deal with this but I knew I did not, under any circumstances want to sleep in that room.

Helen waited until we were all back in the sitting room and then made a polite exit saying she needed to collect some groceries and would fetch me later.

"I can't believe you are here," Mary began. "Do you like my little home?"

I nodded. She was very well spoken with a lovely gentle voice. Again I found it reminded me of a child. There was innocence to her entire manner and yet I felt wary of her, as though she could be quite different if she wanted to be.

"I hope you won't feel badly about me," she continued speaking as she collected a letter from a mahogany desk. "I meant to send this before you left England, but just could not get out to post it. There was so much work to do here cleaning everything before you came."

She handed me the open letter. " You know I love you, don't you?"

It was a strange question. I took the letter and began to read it. "Helen is furious at me for not telling you before," she added.

I began reading it again. It was dated 1st Nov. The letter was written by Mary and in the style of a confession. In it she explained that during her relationship with Roland she had become pregnant by him, eight times. Three babies were aborted and one was miscarried at seven months. This left four live babies all of which she gave up for adoption. John and I it appeared had two more siblings. A girl Mary had called Karen, born in March 1964 and a boy she had named Martin who was born in October 1968.

This was simply too much to take in. I knew that Mary was waiting for some kind of response but I could not think of anything to say. I felt nothing. I could see Mary anxiously waiting for me to indicate that I understood this information and that it did not matter or change anything, but I felt numbed by it. I remember beginning to shiver and realising that the room appeared to be spinning whilst the floor seemed to move away from under my feet. Emotionally it was as though I was removed from my body. "Jet lag" finally got its revenge and I simply could not speak or move.

I woke to Helen's yells. I heard her telling Mary that she would return me in the morning and then I was taken back to Helen's house and put to bed.

CHAPTER EIGHT

SECRETS & SPIES

I had just nine days in New Zealand to get to know my birth mother. This was not easy. Being with Mary was wonderful, I found her witty, intelligent and sensitive. I also learned that there were many different sides to her personality and her behaviour could be extremely unpredictable.

On my second day I woke completely recovered from the jet lag and filled with questions about her disclosure of two further siblings. I was disappointed with this news and I was not sure why except that I kept wondering what other secrets Mary was hiding from me; or whether she might suddenly declare at some time in the future that there were even more children. I needed to know more than anything whether these two siblings were the last.

On arriving at Mary's house though, Helen and I found that Mary had forgotten to take some of her tablets and, as a result she was in a high state of anxiety. Helen quickly ushered her away into a bedroom and closed the door, but I could hear what Mary was yelling.

"Tell her to go away. I don't want her anywhere near me. " She was screaming.

"Well done Mary!" Helen bellowed back. "Can't you even behave for your daughter?"

"Daughter! Daughter! What daughter? I have no daughter. I have no babies. He made sure of that, he took them all away from me." Tell her to go to hell, I don't want the bitch here."

There was no way I could have mentioned anything to do with the "other" babies on this day. Once Mary was composed and safely back on the right dose of medication we spent a pleasant afternoon walking around a Rose Garden in Auckland. I knew I would have to be patient. When Mary was calm she was inspiring to be with. As we wandered around admiring the different species of roses, she calmly removed a tiny pair of scissors from a shoulder bag and with a" snip", took cuttings from several of the plants. Once home, they would be potted and eventually join the masses of plants that filled her garden. She was so quick at this little trick that I found myself quite fascinated by it. When she caught me starring at her, she smiled, revealing a mischievous twinkle in her eye. This Mary was fun.

During the evening she asked whether I would stay at her house the following night. I was not sure. Much as I longed to spend as much time as possible with her, I did not want to be left alone with her. I had not let them know that I had heard Mary's words, but the depth of anger that lived inside her scared me. If I could guarantee she would be stable for that night, then it would be fine.

It was, however, not really an invitation, more of a statement and I knew Mary simply would not understand if I declined her invitation. That evening whilst Helen, her husband Jim and I talked, Helen commented that she would call in very early the morning after my stay in case there were any problems. She advised me not to let Mary drink and to make sure that she ate something.

Mary, it appeared did not eat anything. She did not drink tea or coffee, instead just boiled water with a slice of lemon in it. For her animals though, she cooked. Fresh chicken and meat all prepared and baked until it was soft and tender for them. The animals were the main focus of her home, especially her Bichon, Henry. Henry went with her everywhere and she simply could not exist without him. The dog, rather over weight from over-feeding, resembled a huge, white, grunting marsh mallow.

On our first outing together without Helen, we took Henry. Mary wheeled him along the pavement in a child's antique pram. Up her road, across a main street to a shopping mall. Local residents smiled at her. She smiled back but then always spoke quickly to Henry, as though trying to reassure herself that she could survive an outing.

Once inside the shopping mall, I was left holding the pram as Mary decided that she *had* to buy me a present. The moment Mary was out of sight Henry began to whimper, not a quiet sad little noise, but a slobbering, grunting sort of sound, good and loud, so as to attract people's attention. I remembering saying to as many people who passed by as possible that this wasn't my dog. I was just looking after it for a friend. Friend! This friend was my mother and I was already making excuses about her. It seemed sad to discover that Mary was well known as an eccentric. I did not need to make excuses; people knew both Mary and Henry and were used to the pram. "Your friend is such a special person to us." One lady said as she gave Henry a little pat. " Always brings her baby Henry in this pram. Wouldn't be the same without her." I smiled but wanted to cry.

My birth mother was a "special" person because everyone thought she was completely mad. She was viewed with the same mild amusement as a *bag lady* or the *nutter* on a bus.

"Look what I've bought you," Mary's voice rang out through the Mall. I pushed Henry towards her. In her arms she carried a baby doll. The doll was dressed in a bright pink mock-christening robe.

"This is for you Frannie, my little baby girl. I always wanted a daughter, you know and every daughter should have a dolly…"

I did not say anything. I just stood there dumbly, watching her as she played with the lace on the doll's clothes.

"Look Frannie you can feed it" She began to show me where an attached feeding bottle would be placed. "It's very clever, you'll love this, watch…," she turned the toy upside down to reveal its nappy. Quickly she removed this to show me where the water would eventually come out. " You must remember Frannie to change baby's nappy, we wouldn't want any accidents, would we?" With this she laughed.

"Do you like it Frannie, do you, do you?" Her voice had almost a hysterical note.

"Mary, I am not a little girl anymore. I'm thirty one."

"How dare you speak to your mother like that?" Mary went to raise her hand at my face, but I caught it and instead she began to literally jump up and down with anger.

"You ungrateful bitch…How dare you come here to make fun of me. Oh I know what you think. You think I'm mad. Well, I am…LOOK!" With that she turned the doll upside-down and began to pull its legs off. "Go on, stop me Frannie or I'll break your dolly, I will."

I have never hit anyone before but I did hit Mary. I slapped her across the face. She took a sharp breath inward and stopped jumping around. We stood face to face. I felt dreadful; wanted to go home, this was not the reason I had come to New Zealand.

"I'm sorry," I said. "I'm really sorry."

A small crowd of onlookers had gathered at the disturbance. Mary took hold of the pram and began to walk away from me. I followed. On passing a bin she flung the doll into it and then walked on. We left the Mall, crossed the main road and walked in silence, back to her house.

"You must hate me Frannie," she said as we reached her house. "I wouldn't blame you if you did." There was a question hidden within these statements and I reassured her that I did not hate her, but found her behaviour at the Mall very difficult. "I would never hurt you Frannie," she went on. "I love you, you are my daughter." Mary's voice, like her mother's, had a way of almost disappearing when she became emotional. "I wanted to keep you, you know?"

"I know," I said, but I didn't.

The day passed and night time arrived. I remembered what Helen had said and offered to cook a meal. There was no food in the house at all and so, after much persuasion Mary agreed that I could go to collect a take-away meal. I found a Mac Donald's just a few streets away and brought back two "Kiwi-burgers! Amazing, just the same as any other burger but with the added delight of a thin piece of Kiwi-fruit stuck in the middle. Mary and I had a laugh about this, but she did eat it and so that was the first hurdle over.

The evening passed quickly we just chatted about her life alone and the problems this brought. Much of the time was spent amusing Henry who now thought I was also a Bichon and was competing with me for Mary's attentions.

Eventually I was shown to the fairy-tale bedroom. The bed cover had been pulled back to reveal pure white satin sheets. Soft toys, again bears of all sizes and kinds had been placed over the bed "to keep me company," I said nothing and thanked Mary for the day. We parted with a smile.

For a long while I just sat by the bed gazing out onto her street. Then when I was sure Mary had gone to bed I changed. After removing all the soft toys I climbed into bed. There was a small lamp beside my bed and I decided to keep it lit. It felt safer somehow. I lay there wondering why I felt so uncomfortable about staying overnight in this house. Surely out of all the people in the world I should feel the safest here. Eventually I fell asleep.

A loud bang woke me. It was 2am. Someone was moving around in the house. I climbed out of bed and slowly opened the bedroom door. I could just make out Mary's outline. She was leaning over a kitchen top.

"Is everything alright?" I asked quietly, so as not to frighten her. She did not answer me, but there was a strong smell of Gin.

"Go back to bed Frannie, I just needed some medicine," she did not turn around to face me. I switched on the kitchen light to see her pouring a clear fluid out of a cough medicine bottle.

"Can I help you?" I asked. She turned. Underneath an open dressing gown she wore a tiny see-through red nightie. Quickly she wrapped the dressing gown around her.

"I'm fine, turn off the light. Go back to bed," she said crossly.

I turned off the light but did not go back to my room. "Actually Mary I wonder whether I could have some of your cough medicine. I think I caught a cold on the flight over here," she did not answer. I moved towards her and gently took the bottle out of her hand. "Where do you keep the spoons?" She pointed at a drawer and I fetched one. Then I poured out a spoon of medicine and drank it. Gin, neat and strong.

"My God, that's strong medicine." I choked. "How many spoons will do the trick?"

"What are you doing Frannie?" Mary looked anxious.

"How many spoons of this stuff do I need?"

As she did not answer I poured out another spoon of "medicine" and drank it. Again she did not answer, so I took another spoon, then another.

"Go back to bed!" she yelled. I ignored her and was about to take another spoon of gin when she grabbed the bottle out of my hand.

"You don't understand. I need it. I just need it," she walked away from me and into the sitting room. I followed her.

"Then drink it. Go on or I will."

"Don't be silly. You don't drink," she laughed

"I'll start." I snatched the bottle away from her and poured out another spoon.

"It'll make you ill," Mary said. Her voice was now calm, sounded concerned.

"Fine, then I'll be ill, like you," I replied. I now felt angry. I drank another spoon of the stuff and handed the bottle back. "We'll do this properly." I added. "Where are your glasses?"

Mary collected two glasses and we sat down together. She poured out the contents of the gin into them and we drank them.

"I did love your father," she began. "Dear boy, that's what I called him. I really thought he would marry me." Her voice grew weak. "From a child all I have ever wanted was a husband, some children and a cottage. He did not tell me he was married until after you were born," she paused. "He seemed so kind. He was charming. After having you I did want to leave him but he promised that his divorce would come through soon, so I stayed. I got pregnant again."

Mary stopped talking and stood. She went back to the kitchen and brought back another medicine bottle. " Helen doesn't know about this Frannie, you won't tell, will you?" I shook my head and we both laughed. "God my life was so awful with Ma. Roland promised me a future. He got me my job with a political organisation in London. I did not know he was just using me." She stopped again and drank down a whole glass of gin. I joined her, knowing this was probably an awful mistake.

"Each time I threatened to leave him, he became nasty. God he could rant for hours. He said that the information I was giving him from work could get me into trouble. If I stopped he would inform my boss and kill my babies. I was trapped. I did not know who he was working for but he needed me. I never got any money for the stuff I gave him. He took all the money." Her voice changed

"Sex mad, he was. Always thinking where we could do it. Even worked out the longest stop between train stations and then I would have to allow him to have sex with me," she paused and took hold of my hand. "You were conceived on Finchley common. He raped me."

"Why didn't you use contraceptives?"

"I couldn't take the pill and he wouldn't use a condom. Said he might as well go to a prostitute."

I couldn't think of what to say.

"But Mary you got pregnant eight times. It could not have been rape each time."

She did not answer. She was now standing. She took off her dressing gown and gazed at herself in a wall mirror. "I used to be beautiful you know, really beautiful. Look what he's done to me."

"Mary you look fine," I said as I tried to stand up to comfort her but instead fell headfirst over a coffee table.

"Frannie!" Mary bent down to help me up and I realised that the "cough medicine" was indeed working. On standing I realised that if I didn't find something to eat fast, I would pass out. I made a desperate attempt to reach a tin in the kitchen marked biscuits. I grabbed the tin. Opened it and stuffed a biscuit into my mouth.

Then, tin in hand, I began to make my way back to the sitting room. Mary was standing, starring at me. She was pointing furiously at the tin and looking horrified. I presumed the reason why the biscuit tasted fowl was probably because it had been in the tin for several years. I was wrong. As I made it back to the settee Henry jumped up and began barking loudly.

Mary held him back as I realised that these were not ordinary biscuits, but Henry's special "protein enriched chews."

Mary was now hysterical with laughter and I joined her. In-between bouts of semi-consciousness and bouts of throwing up violently, we laughed and laughed. Everything she said now appeared so funny. The worse the information she gave the more hysterical we became.

Mary told me that Roland had other mistresses and other children by these women. We laughed at the possibility of finding hundreds of missing siblings. We laughed at her fear of him and the abortions she had in order not to have any more children. I remember thinking that this was the real Mary. Not a village idiot at all, in fact quite a clever lady. Playing the eccentric was such a useful tool to use in order to keep people away. We laughed at Henry and his pram and she even confessed that she was always quietly amused at people's reactions to her.

By 7am Mary was slumped over a chair, sleeping peacefully. I was still in the loo, throwing up. Helen arrived and went berserk. Ten minutes later Mary and I sat like two naughty schoolgirls on a settee whilst being read the riot act. Every so often one of us would find Helen's verbal scolding so funny and burst out laughing. This only made Helen angrier. In the end she left saying that we were to "sort" ourselves out by the time she returned.

It did not matter to me any more what Mary had done in her past. Whether Roland had raped her or whether, as was probably the truth, she just could not come to terms with the fact that she had given up four babies for adoption. It did not matter if she had been a spy. None of this mattered. . I had formed a bond with this woman. We had found a unique friendship that evening that would never be taken away.

It struck me that the only way forward was to forget all the reasons why it all happened and to concentrate on finding my other missing siblings. It made me sad to think that we were all parted and missed out on growing up together but I also knew that Mary would not have been a good mother. Although she could be, at times kind and thoughtful, there was a vindictive side to her that was frightening.

The following day we went to the Wanaporoa Peninsula. This is a wonderful stretch of beach set within a conservation area. We took a picnic and sat on a small patch of grass, close to the beach. In front of us, the tide was out, so far out that it appeared to be touching the horizon. Apart from one small group of school children and a few seagulls there was no one there. Helen wanted me to see a little of her Country during my stay and Mary coped well with this particular trip.

On our return, we were all relaxed and I felt confident that Mary was stable enough and trusted me enough for me to tell her that I had met Roland. This was a mistake, a huge mistake. No sooner had I uttered the name "Roland" than she stood and started stomping around the room. Her face had become red with anger.

"You have betrayed me," she yelled. "He'll come and kill me now," she then began to pick up objects and throw them towards me. Helen tried to calm her but it made matters worse.

"Did you know?" Mary asked her. "You did, didn't you? How could you let her come to see me? Are you in touch with Roland too?"

Helen tried everything from being softly spoken and gentle, to shouting back but all with no success. Mary, who had just a few minutes ago been calm and chatty, now stood in front of us, swearing and pulling at her hair. When her mouth ran out of obscene words, she began to roar like a wild animal in pain as she flung herself around the room, spitting and throwing things in all directions. If I had not caused this outburst and had been at a safe distance I would have watched with disbelief that an intelligent human being could behave in this way, but I wasn't a safe distance away and her anger was directed at me. Her voice, usually soft and quite high in its tone, had lowered, changed with her and the words she spat at me contained real hatred.

"I didn't want you, you know," she bellowed. "I didn't want any of you."

I did not react to her words. I did not know how too.

"You bitch," she continued, "you wanted to find out everything, and now you have."

Then she moved towards me and physically pushed me out of her house. She repeated this with Helen and behind us the door slammed shut.

"Leave her," Helen advised. "She'll get over it."

I was angry with myself for being so insensitive. I thought that Mary and I had reached a point where she could trust me. I knew now that this was something she could probably never do. As we made our way down little white steps and through Mary's sweet smelling front garden we could still hear her yells and the sounds of objects being smashed against walls.

We did not return to Mary's that day. The next morning Helen drove me into Auckland and we spent a morning looking around a market. I wanted to enjoy this outing with Helen, we had not spent much time together and it was only her kindness that enabled me to visit Mary. My thoughts were filled with the events of the previous afternoon and Helen tried to reassure me, by explaining that this kind of behaviour was not new to her and that Mary quite frequently expressed herself in this way. I realised what pressure Helen was under, having formed a friendship with Mary and then to receive this kind of treatment. Helen had Jim who often accompanied her on visits to Mary's. In front of a man, Mary never behaved badly, was always charming and witty. It was only when Helen was alone and had forgotten to do something or had done something without Mary's knowledge that the vicious verbal abuse would begin.

"Never get involved with a patient," Helen said as though reminding herself of the rules of nursing. "How could I leave her alone? She had no one. After her uncle's death I should have just walked away, but I liked her, she was different then." Helen paused and tears filled her eyes. "She can be so wicked Frannie, she can say such terrible things and then forget."

I realised that Helen was hoping for more than just a visit from me. This was a way in which she might find an answer for her daily problems of caring for my natural mother. If I were to, somehow have more to do with Mary that would release Helen from the burden she carried. But I had no intentions of moving to New Zealand. Ben would find it almost impossible to find a job in the Aerospace Industry and Mary, in her particular state, not being able to leave her house without persuasion, was very unlikely to ever make it to an airport, let alone England.

If Helen had thought, just for one minute that I would provide a solution to the problem of what to do with Mary, I think it was only now that the reality of the situation sunk in. It was impossible. Mary required quite expert psychiatric help and as she even refused to visit a doctor the thought of introducing a mental health programme was ridiculous.

"I do not know how much longer I will be able to continue like this," Helen added. "I have forgiven her so many times, but her behaviour, even with you here is appalling, I just feel so sorry for you Frannie."

It is true that when I started the search for my natural parents, I was looking for a mother, but this did not apply now as, somehow I had gone past that need. Motherhood had allowed me to become an adult. The reasons I continued to search were partly curiosity but also an intense need to know the truth about Mary and Roland.

Mary had said so much about her life with Roland and yet all the terrible things he was reported to have done did not match the man I met at the Festival Hall. Admittedly one meeting is not enough to see a person's true colours, but his phone calls? They were kind and friendly and in a strange way it was as though he was trying to offer me some fatherly advice.

It was late afternoon before we returned to Mary's house. She did not answer the door and so Helen us in. The place stunk of alcohol. We found Mary bathing Henry.

"Henry's been a naughty boy, Frannie, so he's having a bath."

Mary's voice was high pitched and childlike again. Beside the bath, on a little wooden stool, lay a stick. The dog appeared terrified.

"Henry's had a spanky for being so naughty," she went on.

Helen immediately pushed Mary away from the dog and lifted the creature out of the bath.

"Have you taken your pills, Mary?" Helen asked. Mary bowed her head and as a child caught red-handed, shook it very slowly from side to side. I was handed the dog and the two women disappeared into a bedroom. I dried the animal, which flinched at any sudden move I made. The top of his back left leg was red and swollen.

This was the side of Mary that just did not fit the image of a "victim". It was also the side of her personality that I had sensed would have made her an unfit mother.

Henry was dried and fluffed up and happily eating one of those "chews" when the two women returned. I made some tea and we sat together. Mary was very quiet. The drinking binge she had gone on in our absence now left her sleepy. She apologised for being so angry but was not happy that I had contacted Roland. What seemed to upset her more was the fact I had spoken with Roland's wife, Louise. For some reason she just hated this thought and yet she said repeatedly that she had never met the woman. We talked a little more about Roland and I was surprised by the interest Mary still showed in this man. It was then that she told us that the affair between them had lasted over twenty years. It had only ended when she had left England, in secret in 1979.

Although I still did not understand what exactly Mary and Roland did in their work, Mary had, by revealing the length of their relationship, showed me that she could not have been a victim. It may be true that he had used his charm to win her initially, but to get pregnant so many times and to repeat the process of giving up her babies seemed far more than tragic. With contraception of some kind possible, Mary could have used precautions without Roland ever knowing, but she chose not to and I felt there had to be another reason why she allowed herself to go through these repeated pregnancies. I could not ask her though as whichever way the subject was approached it would imply that she was either stupid, or had got pregnant intentionally.

We did go on a couple more outings but we chose to stay mainly at Mary's home. It made her feel safer and more relaxed. Apart from the unpredictable pill taking and occasional outburst when she felt threatened by a question, she talked about her life. Mary was a person who needed love and yet was unable to trust the love offered.

When we did venture out once more with Henry in his pram I made sure that when people commented on how "special" Mary was to them, I told them I was her daughter. It gave me pleasure to disclose this, much to Mary's amusement. She enjoyed the game playing from the safety of her, nutty as a fruitcake, image. I enjoyed the reaction of people when I said she was my mother. One person even apologised for her comments about Mary. Thought I was her carer. We did have some funny moments.

It was obvious that if Mary could have chosen a different life she would have done so She knew that it was hard to justify some of the things she had done. Giving up four babies was indeed one of the things she could not justify, but it was almost insignificant when compared with the immense damage she must have caused some individuals through her work. She had been a trusted employee of a political organisation and yet with Roland's influence she had, over the years, become his main informant, spying and handing over information to Roland, who then sold the information to interested parties. Apart from the fact that I could never share their political views, I found their work distasteful and shocking. If I had not been her daughter, and someone had told me about her, I would never have wanted to meet this woman.

Now in her late fifties, within the safety of her own home, Mary had time to reflect on her life and actions; time to dwell on the mistakes she had made, the secrets kept even from her own mother.

There is, undoubtedly, strength to this woman. She had survived things that I would not. The guilt, shame and terrible fear she suffers as a result of her actions, now haunts her and imprisons her. The drink, she says, "dulls the pain." It also helps her forget but sadly also awakens the other side of her damaged mind. Mary can move from reality into fiction as though they were one and the same. The hardest thing for her to remember is where reality ends. Her entire life has been wrapped neatly into a carefully constructed web. She has lied to herself, for such a long time; she is simply no longer able to recognise truth.

After just nine days it was time for me to go home. I did not want to leave New Zealand and I did not want to leave Mary. Although she, at times, frightened me, I liked her. There were moments when she was calm and lucid, that I found I was drawn to her quick wit and magnetic character.

Saying "goodbye" was dreadful. Helen, Mary and I all stood in floods of tears at Auckland airport. We hugged and hugged. There was a terrible feeling that I would never see Mary again.

I knew that once home, however often I kept in contact, the physical closeness would be lost and her doubts about me and the terrible paranoia would quickly set back in. If Mary and I lived close it would take years of daily visiting to get really close to her and to help her trust me. Part of my sadness at leaving was that I also knew that once home I simply would be too busy with the daily job of being a mum to spend time playing "trust games "with Mary. I would have to accept that if I was to stay in contact with her, our letters and conversations on the telephone would rely on her emotional and physical state at that time and so most of the time she would be drunk.

My flight was called and we let go of each other for the last time. I promised myself that I would not look back.

CHAPTER NINE

BIRTHS AND DEATHS

On arriving home, the anti-climax of the trip did not last long as I was immediately thrown back into the daily routines of full time motherhood. Toby was now two and a half years old - very advanced in his spoken language but not able to socialise well with other children. The struggle of dealing with this and the constant complaints about his behaviour at the crèche where I was working made me decide to give up this part-time job.

Being a mum to a child who presented unpredictable behaviour was becoming increasingly difficult for me to cope with. Each thing he did had to be watched in case he either hurt himself or another child. He climbed everything he saw, even managing to scale a drainpipe on to an office roof and then declare that he was going to "fly" down. He was rapidly losing contact with his peer group and I was finding it more and more difficult to take him out at all.

I grew increasingly depressed at the constant implications that I was not firm enough with him. Each episode made me question, not only my parenting skills but also whether I had done something dreadfully wrong to this child. Toby was a very much wanted and loved child and yet he showed, at times what I could only describe as disturbed behaviour.

By the time he was four he and I led a completely isolated existence. The only mums that welcomed us into their homes were ones who had a child displaying the same unpredictable behaviour and although I had taken the advice of all relatives that, from time to time visited I could not find a magic solution.

My love for this child was total but I did not understand him and could not seem to find a way of reaching him.

Ben was having to work longer and longer hours and travel more frequently with his job. When at home he would receive a blow-by-blow account from me about what had been going on and so the strain began to affect us all. We decided to seek advice and following a visit to our GP we were referred to see a Paediatrician to have Toby medically examined. Toby was found to have clinical hyperactivity, this did not surprise us, but both Ben and I were completely shocked to learn that added to this Toby was severely hearing impaired.

It was 1994, by now there was a National Register for Adopted People. As I was no longer able to get out so freely to search for information, I chose instead to register both Karen born in 1964 and Martin born in 1968 with the ONS (Office of National Statistics). Their contact register is designed in such a way that if two individuals both place their details with them; they will be cross-matched and placed in contact with one another.

Being an adoptee looking for two adopted siblings meant that it was vital that I registered twice. Firstly in the section that covers someone tracing an adopted person and also in the section of adopted adults searching for birth relatives. Again, it was clear that most searches were designed for one adopted person seeking to be reunited with a birth parent. I wondered how many adoptees where actively searching for other adopted siblings?

Roland was still calling me every other Thursday, although I was growing impatient with him. I could not tell him that I knew about my other two siblings as he was unaware of my contact with Mary, but the conversations between us now was very limited. Not being able to meet up with him or get to know him in person resulted in neither of us feeling confident enough to talk about our emotions. Our chatter was simple and often covered four basic topics. Toby, John, Roland's wife, Louise and our shared interest in writing.

I wanted to know Roland, to understand more about him as a man, not a voice that just reminded me every two weeks that he was somewhere out there. I wanted him to get to know me and to be able to tell me about his relationship with Mary. What he loved about her and how he managed to keep his twenty-year affair with Mary a secret from his wife and children. I wanted to know why they had not used contraceptives? As with much of this search it was so frustrating to be this close to someone and yet still so far away from the truth.

On my birthday in 1994 he called me again and I confronted him about Karen and Martin. He did not say why he had not told me of their existence; in fact he did not say anything. When I said that his silence obviously confirmed that it was true, he just said, as he had done so before' "there is more to Mary than you will ever know." Then I asked him if we would ever be able to meet again and he said "No".

I decided to ask him not to call me again. I remember he asked if I was sure about this and I said. "Yes."

Roland did not call again and it was not until seven years later that I discovered that at the time we were speaking to each other he was gravely ill with cancer and that was the reason he could not leave his home.

Mary remained in contact although I was finding that my own life was complex enough and I was rapidly losing the enthusiasm to question her over her confused statements. Sometimes her letters were sensible and that was great, but every so often Helen would call and say that there had been some crisis and could I telephone Mary. I did not want to be involved in this side of her personality. I found it distressing just to think of her drunk and parading around town drawing attention to herself with her uncontrolled actions and verbal abuse. I did not want to know that she had been arrested for shoplifting or that she had started making nuisance calls to Helen. This was not what I had searched for and certainly something that from my home in Surrey, with my own troubled child, had very little chance of changing.

A ray of hope for my natural family's mental state came in the form of Kate, Mary's elder sister. Since my reunion with Mary she had found the courage to tell her two sisters about her secret babies and Kate had shown an interest in meeting me.

What surprised me about Kate was her sanity. Kate, seven years older than Mary, was a practising magistrate and a senior lecturer at a university in Dorset. Well travelled, with a second home in France and an "academic" as a second husband, she simply did not seem to fit in to this bizarre family.

Ben, Toby and I visited Kate and her husband a few times. The visits were pleasant, I found Kate just as shocked by the story of Mary's life as I was. Kate seemed to have escaped from home much earlier than Mary and being gifted academically had thrown herself into her studies, following a life far removed from her family's affairs. She had managed to distance herself from the family and that made her different. It may have been her way of coping but she really did not seem that interested in Mary or past affairs.

I liked Kate. Like her sister she had masses of dark curly hair and large blue expressive eyes. Also as with Mary, her garden was of great importance to her, but where as Mary had tried to re-create an English rose garden in the humidity of the Auckland air, Kate had managed to grow a jungle in the back garden of her mock-Georgian home in Dorset.

Everything about Kate said that privacy and quiet was of the utmost importance to her. Classical music softly played in the background, books, hundreds of them filled each space within her sitting room and ethnic rugs, beads and sculptures reminded her of years spent working in South Africa.

Kate did not pass judgement on her sister's actions; she just found the whole story baffling and sad. The age gap between them had added to their lack of contact with each other but after our meetings Kate did begin to write more to Mary.

In Oct 1994 I had an ectopic pregnancy. Doctors assured me that I could still get pregnant, with just one remaining tube. I found this difficult to believe but in March 1994 I did become pregnant again. Jonathan was born in January 1995. He arrived just two weeks early and weighed a respectable seven and a half pounds. I only stayed in hospital for six hours and returned home the same day with the new baby. The very next day Toby started school and I managed to keep my promise to him that I would take him on his first morning. It seemed very odd to say goodbye to Toby and then return straight home to start the mothering process all over again with a completely different child.

In April 1995 Mary's mother Lucinda died. She was eighty-five and had been in hospital for some weeks. Mary, unable to make the journey back to England for the funeral, asked me if I would go on her behalf to read some words for her at the service.
"Of course I will," I said. It was only when Mary's "words" arrived that I realised what this meant. I would have to stand up and face my entire natural family on Mary's side and read about Lucinda as though I knew and loved her. I had only met two other members of her family, Andy and one of Mary's sisters, Kate. What would the family make of this? I spoke with Kate who seemed only too happy for me to read. I spoke with John who, far from offering some advice, found the whole thing very funny and said he would accompany me.
"I'm not missing this one." He laughed. "Just imagine their reaction when they find out who you are?
John has a way of dealing with things and immediately took it upon himself to drive all the way from Bolton to Egham and then take me to our grandmother's funeral in Lincoln. This was, (as John always is), a wonderfully generous action and not being able to drive I was grateful, not only for being taken there but also for his company.
However his impulsive actions were slightly compromised by the form of transport he brought for our journey. No longer in the Police Force, he had recently set up his own Antiques Business and so we travelled to Lucinda's funeral in a large, filthy red and white striped lorry that intermittently emitted a cloud of thick black exhaust.

The funeral was held in a tiny church on the outskirts of Lincolnshire. We arrived early in order to find somewhere to change into smart clothes and then made our way to the chapel. Apart from Andy who was busy talking with the vicar, we were the only people there. Andy looked dreadful. The loss of his mother found him almost unable to stand. He bravely attempted a smile and then told me when and where I should stand to read out Mary's words.
A recording of Kathleen Ferrier singing *What is Life?* rang out through the church as members of Lucinda's family walked slowly up

the aisle behind her coffin. About twenty people, all dressed in black, with their heads bowed. Once the coffin had been lowered onto a stand and flowers re-arranged, the family took their places in the pews opposite us. John and I were the only people seated on the left-hand side of the church.

"Didn't the old bat have any friends then?" John whispered. I wondered whether we should promote ourselves, by default, to the right side of the church but the service had started and so we remained in our seats, trying to look inconspicuous.

John kept nudging me and muttering things. "Look at the man in the fifth row. My God, we're related to the Munchkins."

I tried to ignore him. I knew that if I looked at him I would start laughing. Partly nerves and partly because I was terrified at the prospect of having to stand in front of these strangers and read out loud. I was trying to image what I would think if a complete stranger stood up to read at one of our family funerals. It seemed such a bizarre occasion; to being taking part in the funeral of my natural grandmother without anyone knowing who we were. I wondered what it would have been like to have grown up within this family? Where would I be sitting today within this family hierarchy?

It only seemed a few minutes into the service when the vicar announced that as Mary could not be with them, she had asked an "old" friend to read for her. It dawned on me immediately that to be an old friend of Mary's I would need to be in my fifties, not my thirties.

"Go on then woman." John elbowed me out of the pew. "They are all looking at you Fran, get a move on." The smile on John's face was mischievous; he was enjoying every moment of my agony.

I stood and made my way to the front of the church. No one appeared to be looking at me. I began to speak.

I saw Andy look up and was conscious that other family members were now watching as I read out Mary's words. Somehow these words seemed different now. When I had first read them at home they appeared to lack substance, but reading them out loud to the people who loved Lucinda, brought Mary's memories of her mother to life. I felt ashamed to be standing there; it was as though I was intruding in their grief. It should have been someone else reading these words, someone who could feel them and recite them with appropriate sadness.

I wondered if this was Mary's way of letting her family know that we existed. Her small but lasting contribution to her family as when I finished I could see perplexed expressions on the faces of many mourners.

Trying not to look flustered or rushed I made my way slowly back to the pew. John was not laughing; instead he leaned over and whispered.

"I take it we are making a quick get away afterwards?" He said.

"I wasn't that bad, was I?"

"Daggers, Fran, Daggers!"

I did not know what he meant. He pointed to an elderly gentleman in the opposite pew to us.

"You should have seen his face, whilst you were reading. It was as though he'd seen a ghost."

During the prayers I found myself remembering what Lucinda had said to us on our first meeting with her. How when she was in her forties she had thought she was dying and so, expecting the worst, had bought herself a coffin. When some twenty years later she found herself to be still very much alive, she decided to get rid of it. She placed an advertisement in a local newspaper. It read: "For Sale, one coffin, never used, only one careful lady owner."

I couldn't help wondering whether the coffin that sat before us now, was the one Lucinda had chosen all those years ago. She had certainly been quite a character!

When the service was over we followed the procession through North Hykem to a cemetery in Lincoln. The smart line of black limousines, interrupted by John's filthy and somewhat explosive Luton. On reaching the cemetery a groundsman asked John where we were trying to go? John told him and after a somewhat heated exchange of words, we were allowed to pass.

Lucinda was buried on a hill overlooking Lincoln town. Each member of her family threw earth onto the coffin and then silently made their way back to their cars.

"See you at the pub then." Andy grabbed my arm. I smiled but felt very awkward about this.

" Good. See you both there then." Andy continued.

John and I had planned to start our journey home. Even John was now feeling a little embarrassed by the lorry and the thought of having to make up stories about who we were and how we were obviously Lucinda's only friends, did not seem attractive.

There was a group of about ten people in the pub. Andy, his two sisters, Kate and Fiona, (our natural aunts) and their children, (our natural cousins). A couple of Lucinda's cousins and her brother Rupert. He was the old man who had glared at us in church. He had also brought his son.

" I didn't catch your names?" Rupert's son said as we took our seats around three large tables that had been prepared for us.

"Sorry?" I quickly replied, whilst trying desperately hard to think of a way of handling this.

"I thought you read very well." He continued: "How do you know Mary?"

I began to fumble with words when Mary's sister Kate interrupted. "Oh you haven't been introduced." Her voice was loud enough to incorporate all the family members and casual visitors to the pub.

"This is Francesca and her brother John. They are Mary's children."

There was complete silence.

"Do you know" One cousin began. ."I thought as much. It was as though Mary was standing in front of us in church. You are so like her."

I thanked the woman for her comments. She appeared so delighted by this news. "I never knew that Mary had children. For that matter I never knew that Mary got married."

"She didn't,"" John replied. Again there was silence.

"So who's your father?" asked Rupert? His voice was strong and firm. He was not smiling.

"You won't know him," John answered in an equally firm tone. The two men were starring at each other. There was an obvious instant dislike between them. John talks straight; he hates playing games with people. He says things as they are and this is, on the whole, is quite refreshing. Rupert was, however, obviously offended by our presence. I was not sure whether it was because he simply had not been told about us or whether something in John reminded him of someone.

"Tell me your father's name," he demanded.

"His name was Roland," I answered.

At that point Kate interrupted. "Please help yourselves everyone. Come on, let's eat." Rupert did not sit down immediately, instead he stood, his eyes firmly fixed on John. At the mention of Roland's name he appeared shocked. John and I registered this and wanted to question him more but enough had been said.

We ate the sandwiches and I chatted to a cousin, who was my age. She was very excited by our presence and kept saying the news had cheered her up, "quite made her day!"

I would have liked to talk with Mary's other sister, Fiona, but she appeared so frail and timid, that I did not even introduce myself for fear that she would faint. Her daughter remained firmly at her side, seated at the other end of the table; they had absolutely no intention of speaking to us.

Rupert's son spent the entire two-hour lunch studying both John and myself. Every so often I would see him and John starring uncomfortably at each other with Rupert watching over them both, as though waiting for something to happen. Thankfully the conversation revolved mainly around the family's memories of Lucinda and how loyally Andy had cared for her. Once everyone had finished eating John and I prepared to make our exit, feeling it was really time for them to be left to their own private mourning without our presence.

The one thing that was obvious about Mary's family was that they were not close. Lucinda's funeral was the first time they had got together since the last family funeral and it seemed that there were so many secrets that they had kept from one another. It was as though they had gone to the funeral out of a sense of duty rather than to mourn someone they loved.

They all seemed so anxious, so wary of each other as though they were almost frightened of each other. It was certainly a mixed bunch of personalities and characters. This was and never had been a happy family; more one made up of a group of jealous and eccentric individuals who mistrusted each other intensely.

By the chilly response we received from some individuals round those tables, our being there was something that only heightened the tension between them all. Why Rupert and his son, and Fiona and her daughter seemed so hostile, I did not know. None of them were close to Mary, indeed only her sister Kate kept in contact with her and she was the only person that was truly welcoming towards us.

It was only when I was saying goodbye to Andy that he, somewhat inappropriately, I thought, mentioned that Lucinda's Will had made him the sole beneficiary. I didn't understand why he was telling me this; I just assumed it was drink talking. John, however, could not make his escape from the pub fast enough. When I caught up with him he was waiting for me in the Luton.

"Well, we've really caused a stir this time, Fran." John was laughing so much I could not make sense of what he was saying.

"Do you think we have upset them?" I asked.

"Oh yes. Wouldn't have missed this for the world."

John was supposed to drop me off at Lincoln train station but he was so enjoying his new found understanding of his natural relatives, he decided to drive me all the way home.

"You haven't worked it out yet, have you?" John continued. "You poor simple creature. You think they are upset by the fact that Mary had two illegitimate children, don't you?"

I wasn't sure what I thought but I knew John would enlighten me once he had recovered from the pleasure his knowledge was bringing him.

"Money." He glanced my way. "They think we are after the family fortune." Again he dissolved into raucous laughter. "Brilliant! They are terrified we've come to stake our claim to the family inheritance."

"You're joking," I answered, realising that it did make sense.

"I can just see them now all sitting where we left them, thinking that they are going to have to hand part of their good fortune to us and worrying about it all."

"But John, Andy says Lucinda's left all her money to him."

John roared with laughter. "Brilliant. Those sad bastards, all paying their last respects……….my foot! The only reason they went to the old witch's funeral was to make sure she was good and dead and that they could get whatever they could get from her."

John and I laughed nearly all the way home.

"You know, I think Mary has a sense of humour after all. What a brilliant way to get her own back on that bunch of misfits. Can you imagine growing up within that family"?

It was a sobering thought and yet, at that point, it just seemed hilarious.

John's upbringing left him feeling as though he did not belong to any family. Our reunion brought him a chance to create a family of his own and when he later, met and married Sue, she brought with her the emotional stability that he craved for as a young man.

Over the last ten years our relationship has become close. We have been blessed with the opportunity of sharing events and finding new relatives together. All these things have help us to form a history together.

In late April 1996, exactly one year after Lucinda's death, I received a letter from the Office of National Statistics. My sister Karen had placed her details with them and we had been cross-matched. The letter gave her telephone number and I rang it.

"Karen?" I asked.

"No, sorry Karen's at work. This is her mum, can I help?"

I was going to end the call by saying I would call later, but the lady interrupted. "Is that Francesca?"

I was surprised that she knew.

"We've been expecting your call. So wonderful for Karen. Oh she will be pleased. The poor girl's had such a bad time."

Karen's mum began to talk about Karen in a way that someone does when trying to prove that person is upright and honest. She wanted me to approve of my newfound sister.

Karen's mum is a devoted mother and I was pleased for Karen that she had a close relationship with her. It transpired that Karen's parents had split up when she was only two years old and some years later her mother had married again. Karen's stepfather, however, had sexually abused her throughout her childhood. The marriage had ended but not before much damage was done.

CHAPTER TEN

FOUND AND LOST

Karen had known of my existence for many years. She had also known about John and Martin. On her adoption file, given to her by her adopted father was a list of all our birth names and birth dates. Her adopted father had, at sometime, made some investigations of his own and managed to uncover the fact that Mary had four babies, all placed within different families.

Karen had started her own search in 1989, the year I moved from Windsor to Egham. She had used NORCAP (National Organisation for the Counselling of Adoptees and their Parents) to help her find me. Unfortunately I had just dropped my membership with them as I had no knowledge, at that time, of any further siblings and had already been reunited with John. It was only a matter of one month's difference between my moving house and NORCAP trying to establish contact, but it resulted in them not being able to trace my new address and so Karen's search had not progressed.

If Karen had successfully traced me it would have been just three years after I had found John and the three of us would by 1996 have known each other for seven years. Unfortunately, this did not happen. I was able to tell her that John and I had been in contact since 1986 and that I had not known about her or Martin until 1992.

Karen was delighted that John had been found. She explained that she had never searched in order to find her birth parents; instead she was only looking for her own peer group, especially her older brother.

At first I did not understand why an older brother? She explained that because her adopted parents had divorced when she was only two years old; they had not adopted any further children and therefore she had grown up without any siblings. Being an only child she always believed that if an older brother had been around he would have protected her from her stepfather's advances.

People search for all kinds of reasons and this was one of the saddest I had heard. I was, however, unsure about Karen's expectations now, as the abuse was over and some fifteen years had lapsed since. Now, as a married woman, with two children of her own, her wish had been granted and she did indeed have an older brother but one who was completely unconnected to her emotionally and one that had his own expectations.

It became clear that when John had telephoned Karen to introduce himself, he had found her story most disturbing and one that he had not wanted to hear during an initial conversation. John and I decided the best move forward would be to meet our sister before any more was said.

On May 16 1996 at a pub in St. Albans, John and I were reunited with Karen. We picked this meeting point as being neutral territory and one that was more central to Lancashire, Surrey and Essex.

John, his wife Sue, Ben, his sister Emma, Toby, Jonathan and myself all arrived at the pub early and found a table outside in the sunshine. It was a gloriously warm day for May and as we ordered drinks and played with the children there was a feeling of relaxed anticipation. This was again a huge breakthrough in a search that was now eighteen years old and still continuing. It was only the fact that both Karen and I had placed our names on both parts of the National Contact Register with the ONS (Office of National Statistics), that this meeting was possible. Without the ONS contact register and without the knowledge that such a register exists, there was, and still is, ridiculously little provision made for reuniting adopted siblings separated at birth.

A car drove into the pub car park and John raced over to meet it. As I followed him I watched and saw my sister climb out of the car and embrace John. It was like looking at Mary. The physical similarity between Karen and Mary was astonishing. Both these ladies are tall, around five foot eight/nine inches. Both have dark, wavy hair and large blue eyes, but the thing that was so striking was that both Karen and Mary have identical voices and identical "walks." Both women carry themselves very well, very upright with straight back and shoulders. It was quite remarkable to see that deportment alone could prove Karen's identity. I was quite astounded by the likeness between them. Although I know some of my facial features are similar to Mary's I did not get the same height or colouring.

Coupled with the walk, was also the build. Both Karen and Mary have identical builds, both broad across the shoulders. Karen and I embraced and laughed with the relief of meeting. Then she introduced us to her husband Gareth and their two children, Stuart who was five, one year younger than Toby and Lucy who was nearly two, just six months older than Jonathan.

This reunion was different from all the others because we were not just two individuals meeting for the first time. We were two families, sisters, brothers, and brother in laws, sister in laws and cousins. Each person, whether adult or child was meeting for the first time a new relative and so the stress and anxiety of a one to one reunion was, after the initial greetings, removed instantly.

One other thing that also added to the enjoyment of that day was the fact that we all met on neutral territory. A pub, on a spring day, with swings for the children and a relaxing environment for the adults. The tension that someone's home can bring is, in comparison, quite noticeable. You cannot speak so freely within another person's territory, there are boundaries. Here, in the open air, there was space, not only to move around freely but space to chat with who ever you chose to.

To an outside observer we would have appeared as a group of old friends who were simply sharing a day together. There was nothing to indicate quite how unique this occasion was. Karen, John and I chatted as though we had all known each other for years. The only thing was that we hadn't and although, in company we got on well, on returning home there was the feeling that some things had not been said.

John and I talked at length about the delight we felt at meeting Karen and wanting to see her again. We knew that it was important that she did not feel left out or intimidated by the fact that we had already formed a bond.

It is true that John and I have over the years grown close; we are alike and able to joke and argue much as siblings do. We also had one advantage, we had both grown up with a sibling and that had given us the experience to understand the love, hate, jealously and envy that exists, at times, between all brothers and sisters. The relationship was clear and one that had not, up until now been explored for its meaning. Karen had made it clear that she had wanted to find her older brother most of all and John, just one year and fifteen days older than her, fitted the description. Not only her older brother but at six foot, five and half inches tall he was, quite literally, her big, older brother.

As we lived quite far away from each other it was normally only possible for two out the three of us to get together at one time. Life styles, our own family commitments and children all made it difficult to spend time together but also our individual expectations played a large part in deciding who met up with who and what was discussed.

I have always wanted to know all there is about each natural relative I have found. John, although openly stating that he does not wish to have contact with Mary, also is keen to know about all family members and the arrival of Karen brought him another sister, another brother-in-law, another nephew and niece.

Karen, although curious about the circumstances surrounding Mary and Roland, did not want to have any contact with them. She was very clear about her need to be close to a brother and although whilst, in her company we got on well, there was also a sadness that she had not been able to share the same time with John, as I had done.

We moved into an interesting time of what I presume was a form of sibling rivalry. John, the brother between his two sisters. This was a new experience and strange because instead of establishing our natural hierarchy within the family at four of five years old, we were going through the process whilst in our mid to late thirties. In 1998 we had moved away from Egham and now lived in a delightful, but rather dilapidated farmhouse in Newbury.

Toby now eight, had undergone several operations to place grommets in his ears, but far from this resulting in a calmer happier child, he was still displaying considerable hyperactivity and a constant frustration with life. Settling in to our new home and starting a new school took Toby about a year to get used to but, without the labels that had been attached to him back in the small town in Surrey, he began to make friends and seemed to enjoy living in a larger, busier town.

When I had, over the years, mentioned to Mary about Toby's hyperactivity, she had often commented on how one of Roland's children had been "just like that!" She always said that he had grown out of it, as he became older. This information was comforting to hear and because of that I never thought to ask her how she knew so much about it. I assumed that Roland probably talked to Mary about his home life.
I was to discover later on that this was not how Mary knew so much about Roland's children.

By 1999 we were getting quite involved in community life in Newbury. Ben still made a long journey to work and back each day and I had started a counselling training course.
 John and I still got together often but we found it hard to get to know Karen. She was not as happy to let down her barriers and disclose her thoughts to us.
I kept being reminded of how as a young girl I had two particularly close friends. Although we all lived within two roads of each other, we never played together. For a while I played with one and then found I was playing with the other and then as the tables turned I would not see either of my two friends for a while, as they got together. This was all part of growing up and always involved much tale -telling of the excluded one.

For many years this pattern continued as one of us would fall out with one other and so on and then, as children do, make it up again and become best friends.
What we were doing as children was learning to accept each other's individuality. The friendships formed between us grew with an understanding of each other and then as adults because of the history we had between us.

I had the strong feeling that something similar was happening between John, Karen and myself. Somehow we were playing each other off against the other.

I was quite hurt by the fact that Karen had declared so early on in our contact making that she was looking primarily for a brother. Although I could understand her reasons, they now dated back to her childhood and yet she had retained the same reasons for searching throughout her twenties.

Karen had known that there were four of us before she began to search and so had searched only in order to find her own peer group. On thinking about this I wondered if the emphasis of my search would have been different if I had always known I had brothers and a sister.

I was also dismayed by the fact that both Karen and John did not want to have a relationship with Mary. I could not understand how they did not share any of the curiosity that I had about our birth parents. What was interesting was the fact that they both felt their own peer group was the priority here. Karen was concerned about her adopted mother and felt it would be wrong to establish a relationship with Mary. John listened when I talked about Mary but did not know what he wanted say to her and so has never managed to keep up any contact.

As a child I never gave any thought to having natural siblings, it just did not exist, even as a concept. Perhaps I had not placed enough priority with my own siblings and their own thoughts about their adoptions. Certainly I was surprised at the negative way in which both Karen and John viewed Mary. They saw her, not as their birth mother, but as the woman who gave them up. Mary was not someone either of them would be comfortable knowing and so, for them, she was not a priority in their individual searches.

Karen's need to have a brother was fulfilled by John making several visits to her. As John established a relationship with Karen and her family I hoped that she and I might find a bond. Certainly when we spent time together I found we shared the same sense of humour and having children of similar ages did give us something in common to talk about.

Having the children always around during get-togethers also meant that sometimes the conversation was guarded and so Karen and I decided it might be a good idea to go away on a weekend together, without the husbands or kids. It was decided that it would be quite fun to each take our best female friend, someone who had known each one of us for several years and therefore be able to add some missing history when needed. It would also keep the weekend light-hearted and fun.

My friend, one of the two girls from my youth, had a house in Hastings and so we decided to go there. Although it was a fun weekend with walks along the beach, meals out in the Old Town and two extremely late nights of chatting over the memories Karen's friend had about her as a child and my friend had about me, it was also, for me, quite sad.

I had not considered the impact that missing a history together has on natural relatives. Karen and her friend giggled and chatted over Karen's childhood with the sudden shrieks of "Oh no don't say that." Or "Oh god I remember him" followed by squeals of laughter as the memories they shared came flooding back. Similarly my friend Clare and I did the same thing and although the stories told between us four women were funny, almost hysterically so at times, they belonged to our very separate lives.

As I watched them I realised that the sister was the person who had shared Karen's childhood, grown up with her, gone out with her choosing clothes, going to parties and shared Karen's sad moments and innermost thoughts. Anna was, by all accounts, a sister to Karen. They might not be related by blood but the body language and expressions they used between them, often without the need for words highlighted an intimacy to their friendship that can only be shared by two people who have grown up together.

The same could be said of Clare and I and it struck me that although, as women Karen and I could be friends, maybe even good friends we would never cross the bridge from friendship to being sisters as the years, it takes to place "foundations" would always be missing. I did not know whether this problem greater because we were of the same sex. I had not experienced this problem with John and perhaps it is easier to establish bonds with someone of the opposite sex.

After the weekend away there was quite a time of no communication between Karen and I. John still visited both of us and passed information between us. I felt that part of the problem between Karen, John and myself was that we were three. As with the two friends I shared when a girl, three is an odd number and like it or not, one person is left slightly on the sidelines. I believed that an answer might be found if the numbers were evened up so decided to ask NORCAP to help me search for the last sibling, Martin.

I thought that if John had a brother and someone of his own sex to relate to then Karen would not only have a choice of brothers, but also not be the *new* girl anymore. I felt whichever way it went it would not cause harm.

NORCAP, not only gives advice to all parties involved in adoption, but also has a Contact Register and a very well needed *voice* when it comes to the rights of adopted people. They also provide the services of trained counsellors and run an intermediary service. It was this intermediary service that I was to experience in my search for Martin. NORCAP took up the search and provided me with an intermediary who would liase between Martin and myself.

It did not take long to find Martin and the intermediary telephoned to explain that she would forward a letter to his last known home address and hopefully it would be forwarded to him. A couple of weeks later and she called me again to say that she had just had a wonderful chat with my brother. Martin had given her permission to hand over his details to me and so I telephoned him. I had never, up until this point, given any thought to what it must be like to be found.

Martin, the youngest of us all at thirty, was seven years younger than me and went from believing that he had one half-sister to being told that he had two full-blood sisters and one full-blood brother. Not only that but if he wanted to know about his natural parents the information was at hand. We arranged for him and his wife to come over to our house. John wanted to be there but I felt it was best that Martin met only one relative on his first visit.

Martin was prompt and greeted me politely. There was a strong sense that he was in full control of his emotions; it was so different from my reunion with John. Martin, six foot, eight inches tall, slim and handsome, did physically resemble John and I remember laughing at the fact that he was even taller than John was and wishing John had been there.

There was also, however a huge difference in the way in which Martin expressed himself. He was calm to the point of being almost unemotional about the whole thing. His wife, although friendly, seemed wary and somewhat reluctant about all these newfound relatives. Ben sensing the unease decided to take children out, leaving us to talk alone for an hour or so. When I am nervous I talk a lot. As I talk a lot anyway this means I generally get an attack of verbal diarrhoea. I had offered them drinks and supplied biscuits and generally chatted away about various members of the natural family. It only dawned on me about twenty minutes later that Martin had not made one enquiry. He did not seem to ask anything.

Apologising for my babbling I asked him if he would like to see a picture of Mary. He did not know, seemed hesitant, yet curious. I decided not to press the issue and asked him about himself.

He was very quick to talk about his adopted family, as his family. He talked about his childhood and his father and mother and sister. He talked about his education and obvious academic ability and his career. He had made it clear that his family were the people who raised him. And I was curious to know why he had bothered to allow me to make contact with him.

He explained that he was a diabetic and he was interested to know if his diabetes was heredity. I said that I did not know but could find out, this seemed to please him.

Then he suddenly decided he did want to see a picture of Mary and so I collected one. He took the picture and studied it. He did not say a word, just stared at it and then placed it, face down on the side. Just when I felt that he was beginning to relax, Ben arrived back with the kids and it was as though Martin remembered that he did not want to ask anything.

The atmosphere was calm, but underlying it was the feeling that Martin had not wanted to be found, as though he might or might not have decided one day to search. That choice had now been removed and he was not in control of the knowledge he might receive.

The use of an intermediary is for exactly that reason. To give the person being traced an opportunity to say they do not wish to have any contact. In reality I feel that once you have been given the choice it is almost impossible not to want to *know something*. It is like being told only half of a secret. You know you should not hear the rest, but curiosity is a strong force.

I felt that I had been insensitive to Martin, by assuming that he would be interested in knowing about his natural parents. The premise that he wanted contact with me allowed my enthusiasm to run away with me and I had not given enough thought to his expectations or possible reasons for coming to meet me.

It is apparent that the expectations of all four of us have been different to each other. Not so much in the desire to meet with each other and get to know one another but for our reasons to meet and for our individual curiosity in different areas related to adoption.

My original search was for Mary and even though I know she would not have been a good mother I also realise, that if she had not lived out her life in the way she did, I would not be alive. For my life alone, I am grateful to her.

John and Karen make me question my reasons for remaining in contact with her. They are probably right when they remind me that Mary gave away four babies and that she was obviously someone with little or no morals.

I have learned (slowly) over the years that it is better not to bombard my siblings with the latest saga in New Zealand or to talk much about Mary. If she were in the U.K. it may be different as I would undoubtedly be visiting her regularly and then the curiosity may get the better of them. New Zealand is a safe distance and in many ways I can appreciate both Karen and John's views.

Martin knows that if he wishes to have any contact with her he can ask for her address. During the last two years I have not seen Martin. The last time I saw him was Mothering Sunday 2000. This was the first and only time all four of us siblings, have been together.

Since then I have not seen him. Martin and Karen have formed a relationship and so I occasionally get news about him from her. I am pleased that Martin has decided to stay in contact with at least one of us and that he made that choice freely. I am also pleased that Karen at last has a brother, with whom she is able to make memories.

If we had been a family who had grown up together the bonds may have been different. It is interesting though that as a family, without history, we have as adults still made conscious or unconscious decisions over who we are more likely to get on with.

In truth my search should have ended here. Certainly I had finished what I had set out to do and managed to trace and reunite all four siblings.

Being in contact with Mary, though, left many questions unanswered. There was so much confusion over what Mary's life had actually been like and why she had stayed with Roland for so long. Also with my siblings not wanting contact with her I wanted to find out the truth partly to see if there would be something positive, about Mary that might enable them to feel they could change their minds.

I had broken off contact with Roland in 1994. I had told him not to telephone me again, as he was always unable to meet with me and had not told me about Karen and Martin. I had no way of making contact with him, as he had never given me his address. In 2000 I had begun using a computer and found a site simply called *People Finder*. This fascinated me and also made me realise just how easy it would have been to trace people if the technology had existed at the time I began my search. I started to play about looking up people I knew. Then I decided to try and trace Roland

When we had been in contact he used to give me little snippets of information, like clues in a puzzle they now had to be put together. I knew that he had five children of his own. Four boys and one girl. I knew that one of his sons lived close to him and one was disabled and lived with him. Where? I did not know other than he had said Hampshire. The old address that Mary had given me was a Kent address, but Roland had definitely said he was somewhere near Basingstoke.

It took just four minutes on the computer to trace an address. It was not Roland's but his son. His eldest son Don. Up popped the address and he was the only one of that name listed. I did not want to contact Don. That would quite possibly open a can of worms and he most likely did not know of my existence. I punched in Roland's surname for Kent and immediately another address popped up. Again not for Roland, but for his wife, Louise. I then checked the Electoral register and found there was no listing for Roland. I suspected he might have died. I decided to call his wife.

CHAPTER ELEVEN

BEHIND CLOSED DOORS

"Hello, is that Louise?" I asked.

"Yes." The voice sounded familiar, it was the same woman that I had spoken with over eight years ago.

" I'm sorry to bother you," I said, "but I need to find out where Roland is?"

"He's dead," Louise replied abruptly "Died four years ago. Who is this please?" Her question sent terror through me. It is the one question I never quite know how to answer sensitively.

"My name is Francesca. I spoke with you several years ago concerning a young man who was trying to trace his father."

"Yes I remember. What do you want?" Louise's voice did not sound as cold as I remembered it was almost friendly. I knew that I would probably never get another opportunity to speak with this lady again. Being the daughter of her late husband's mistress did not place me at the top of her list of people to confide in and so I decided to explain right then, exactly who I was and why I need the information about Roland. I chose to make medical history the main reason for needing to find out more about him.

"Who is your mother?" the question came back without hesitation.

"You have never met her," I replied. "It does not matter who my mother is."

Louise asked again and so I told her. "Mary Brown."

"Mary!" Louise, obviously surprised, paused for a moment. "Are you sure?"

"Yes."

"But that is impossible. I would have known if Mary had become pregnant." There was another pause as though Louise was trying hard to remember. I waited.

"You say there are four of you?"

"Yes," I replied, knowing this to be horrible news to give someone and feeling dreadful that I had told her.

"When? When did Mary have you all? I want to know the dates."

" I was born in 1961. John in 1963, a girl in 1964 and another boy in 1968."

Again there was silence.

"Well," Louise sighed, "I suspected there was one baby..." She paused. "But four! And you say that Roland is father to all of you."

"Yes," I replied and then found myself apologising to her, not only for breaking this news but also for my own existence. Louise was quick to say that there was no need to apologise, that it wasn't my fault, but I was trying to imagine just how I would feel if Ben had four children by a mistress. I wasn't sure I could cope with the enormity of the secret.

Whilst I was realising just how devastating this news must be for Louise, she began to tell me that I should never feel responsible for what had happened and that she could not believe that two people would give up four babies.

I was completely stunned by this woman's generosity and kindness. It was as though I was confiding in a close friend about a particularly sensitive problem. Her reaction was completely selfless.

"Mary was my friend." Louise began. "For many years she and I were close. I never knew why she left or where she had gone. Is she still alive?"

This sentence left me speechless. Mary had always said quite clearly that she had never met Louise. Now Louise was saying something quite different and although it did not make sense I felt that I was, at last getting close to the truth.

"When did you meet Mary?" I asked

"She was working in a book shop when Roland met her. She was having a terrible life at home and so Roland invited her to tea with us. From then on we became friends, best friends. I cannot believe that she would have a baby without me knowing. Mary stayed with us often, even came on holiday with us, she was part of the family. When I was taken ill and had to go into hospital she even looked after my children."

So this was why Mary had been so upset at the thought of me speaking to Roland. Mary knew that if contact were made with Louise her story would change dimension. She could no longer play at being an innocent victim.

I was angry with Mary, for now I had done something really dreadful. Through Mary's lies I had thought it was safe to speak with Louise. Whether or not she ever suspected anything, Louise now knew that her husband and her best friend had had an affair. To add injury to insult Louise was also made to realise that for twenty years the two of them had betrayed her.

To add the final blow to this dreadful news, if Louise ever doubted the reality of her situation, the proof of her husband's extra-marital interests, existed in the form of the four, now adult children produced during that secret affair.

It became clear that during those twenty years Mary had worked her way into the family home as a person who could be trusted. Louise often alone and with five children to care for and very little money to live on had accepted her and trusted her as a close friend.

It was at this point of the conversation that I felt ashamed to be Mary's daughter. I understood at last. The whole sorry tale was not really centred on the work Roland and Mary did together, although that was undoubtedly controversial. It was, in fact, far simpler. Mary had wanted Roland and she had wanted him more than anything else.

During the next week I received a letter from Louise which contained not only a details of Roland's life but also photographs of Roland and Mary that Louise had taken. The photo's always pictured them together, his arm around her shoulder as friends do.

I thought of Louise and wondered how she was coping with all this news. She had been married to Roland for over fifty years and had cared for him, right up until his death from cancer in 1995 and now she cared full-time for one disabled son. It seemed to me that this woman had been very wronged and I had opened many wounds. I did not want to upset Louise with any more contact. Her kindness to me was amazing and she said she would speak with her eldest son about it all.

A year passed and at Christmas I sent Louise a card. Although I had her eldest son's address and phone number from an Internet site, I felt that I should wait until Louise had spoken with him first. I had not thought about the possibility of meeting any more of my siblings. I had always thought that they would not want to know any of us because we symbolised their father's infidelities.

The months rolled by and I still did not hear from Louise. I was still writing regularly to Mary and telephoning every three months or so. One night Mary phoned and as I listened to her talk about the troubles she had with her animals; my patience ran out and I told her that I was in contact with Louise and asked her why she had not told me they were such close friends.

Typically unpredictable, Mary did not deny anything, instead launched in to a long talk about how difficult it had been keeping the affair secret from Louise. When she had been pregnant with John she had gone into labour at Roland's house. Roland had told Louise that Mary had kidney problems and so he was *just* going to take her to hospital.

At that time Roland lived in Kent. He proceeded to try and drive Mary to Windermere, wanting the child to be born there but they got caught short in Lancashire and Mary gave birth to John in Bolton, the town where Roland had grown up. After the birth he took Mary and the baby to his mother's house where Mary stayed until the baby was given up for adoption. Roland somehow managed to explain all this away, not only to his wife but also to his mother.

The ability to conceal a pregnancy is well known and being less than five pounds at birth I was probably quite easy to conceal. John was six pounds and so with loose clothing and careful planning he too was maybe not that obvious. Karen, however, weighed nine pounds at birth and Martin was over ten pounds. The most extraordinary thing is that no one ever suspected any of Mary's pregnancies.

Roland and Mary managed to keep their work, their lives and their children secret and in the end it came to nothing as Mary finally realised that Roland would never leave his wife and children and so her obsessional love for this man changed into an obsessional hatred. Over the years this hatred had become further twisted with a bitterness that grew within her and slowly ate away at her, causing her to question the choices she had made. The reality of Mary's life was far too much for her to deal with and so she coped by fabricating the truth and denying to herself any responsibility for her actions, choosing instead to believe that she was a victim.

When she left the country in 1979 (coincidentally the same year as I began searching), she went to live with her uncle. It was by chance that this uncle visited England in that year and came to stay with his sister, Lucinda, Mary's mother. Mary had remembered him from when she was a young child. He had, at that time, taken her for a walk, bought her an ice cream and shown her kindness by listening to her and although she was only five years old she had declared that she would marry him one day.

This uncle's return at the point when Mary had finally decided she wanted to get away from Roland could not have been timed better. As when she was five years old, he again listened to her as she told him the whole story and, like a true Knight in Shining Armour, he rescued her by taking her back to New Zealand with him. He was already divorced and living alone.

Together they created a completely private world, not speaking with anyone outside the four walls of their home and never being apart from one another. For the next seven years they shared every moment of their daily lives. Mary filled her uncle's house with frilly curtains and cushions, brought a variety of animals into his home and threw herself into creating her English garden. For the first time in her life Mary experienced equality within a relationship. It was the ultimate in obsessional relationships and yet this time it was a mutual obsession. Roland did try to find Mary but the uncle protected her and after a while Roland stopped calling.

This incredibly intense relationship brought Mary fulfilment and sense of purpose in her life. It also brought home the reality of the life she had lost and the price she had paid, both physically and emotionally for the love of one man. During her life with her uncle she began to drink. It helped her cope with her memories but it also muddled her thoughts and her dreams.

When, in 1986 her uncle was diagnosed with lung cancer, Mary nursed him and cared for him until his death in 1987. After his death she had gone into mourning, not only for her uncle, but also for her life with Roland and her lost babies. The bottle replaced companionship and anxiety, panic attacks, agoraphobia, and a host of daily rituals prevented her from leaving her home at all.

Helen had entered Mary's life at this point and tried to help. For ten years these two ladies were friends. Helen had broken a fundamental rule of nursing; not to get involved, but Helen had seen something in Mary that she liked and thought it safe. For a few years the friendship was strong and Mary disclosed to Helen much of her sad tale, always putting herself into the victim's shoes, making Helen believe that Roland was cruel to her and that she was *forced* to stay with him.

Helen was taken in completely by this until I made contact with Mary, then the first seed of doubt was placed into Helen's mind. Some parts of Mary's story did not make sense.

As Helen began to suspect that Mary was hiding information from her, Mary was becoming more possessive about her friendship with Helen, phoning her each day, often three or four times to check up on her whereabouts. Questioning her about her friends and work and suddenly needing her at all hours of the day and night. Mary was, in effect transferring the dependency she had on her uncle over to Helen and although Helen could see it happening there was nothing she could do to prevent the process roller coasting. By the early 1990's Helen was not only Mary's only friend, but having to be *on call* twenty-four hours a day to deal with the severity of Mary's mental illness.

Helen had seen my trip to New Zealand as a possible answer. Maybe Mary would "snap" out of her varied mental state and even contemplate returning to England. What Helen and I had failed to realise was that I was simply not a significant part of Mary's life.

Getting pregnant was the way in which Mary saw a possibility of "winning" Roland. It was not the babies that she wanted, it was the man and so once each baby had been given up, she seemed to simply repeat the pattern over and over again, believing each time, that Roland would, leave his wife and go to her.

When I was looking for Martin and using the services of a NORCAP intermediary I remember that during one of our telephone discussions she asked me if Mary had "learning difficulties."

I laughed and asked her why on earth she wondered this? Her reply was that although she had heard of a couple of cases where a woman had given up more than one child for adoption, she had never heard of anyone having four "accidental" babies.

I didn't like to tell her that Mary had, in fact, become pregnant by Roland eight times.

It is truly extraordinary that Mary allowed herself to become pregnant so many times and not think of using any form of contraceptives. When I have breached the subject with her she always referred the problem to Roland and his view of women.

"Said he might as well go with a prostitute." Her answer implied that the responsibility for the pregnancies was born from Roland's misguided association between safe sex and prostitution.

It is true that Mary alone was not responsible for our births, although she is the only one who is mentioned on our birth certificates, Roland was equally responsible. It is strange how the intermediary did not asked whether he might have had learning difficulties, as being a married man, with five children within that union, makes me wonder what he really thought about all of us, his illegitimate babies. Did we matter to him or was he just as obsessed with Mary as she was with him?

Louise was painting a picture of a good man who was a kind father to their children. If he had been any different to this, would she have told me? I did not know.

The year 2000 was the first year since 1979 that I had not been actively searching for anyone. The search had taken some twenty years to complete and should have ended here as I had found all my, full blood, natural relatives.

For the first time ever I did not have any urge to find out more. Louise had either not spoken with her eldest son or he quite simply did not want to make any contact. I did not have any desire or need to know Roland's children; I was completely wrapped up in my own children and their immediate needs.

In July of this year Toby went into hospital to have a five-hour operation to remove a Cholesteotoma from his left ear. This dead-skin growth had over the year eroded away all of his inner ear bones, leaving him almost completely deaf in that ear. It was, in fact only by accident that the growth was discovered at a routine ear check. The result was a terrible build up of anxiety prior to the operation and then, once it was performed and a new eardrum constructed, a long period of recovery.

For Toby this meant a whole summer of no physical activities of any kind. Being a child who was not only hyperactive but also, active in all kinds of sports, resulted in a very long and difficult summer.

In September of that year Toby's operation was declared a success and with my younger son, Jonathan starting school, the prospect of having a little time to myself seemed delicious. Time to think or try my hand at some creative writing, things that I had enjoyed before having children seemed possible once more. There was, however a problem that was growing and with my days taken up watching over the children, I had chosen to ignore the obvious signs that all was not well with Ben. I assumed that Ben would be able to sort out any problems he had in his usual silent way. I was wrong. Three weeks into the new school term Ben became very ill, through stress at work and undoubtedly stress at home. The result was that he was suddenly unable to work.

Years of deadlines, targets, travel, extra hours, working weekends all finally caught up with him and the result was a total *melt down*. Ben was so ill that, at first, he slept for most of the day. When awake he would sit for hours, not speaking or reading, just quietly sitting as though daydreaming.

I felt completely out of my depth with this and although our doctor was sympathetic and prescribed some *happy pills* the reality was that they did not work as an instant cure and Ben was far from feeling happy. We were all emotionally, reaching rock bottom and having to lie to relatives so they wouldn't know that Ben was not working. Ben was convinced that no one would understand and so we didn't refer to his problem as a breakdown, just said he was suffering with stress.

On the eighth of November my mother telephoned me to say that she was worried as my father had gone out for the day and had not returned. It was six o'clock and I told her not to worry, just to call me if he had not returned by six-thirty.

My father was now eighty-five, registered blind and deaf, and no longer able to read or study. Instead he filled his days with bread making, cooking, walking and enjoying a number of classes on History. On that day he had gone with a group into London to Docklands and was not due home until after five. Normally I would phone him each day around four to catch up with news and to just have a chat.

When six- thirty came I telephoned mum. The first thing I heard was the sound of radio four booming out in the background and knew instantly that he must have arrived home safely. It was a lovely conversation as dad quite enjoyed the thought that his daughter was "checking" up on him. I remember he was laughing at the thought of me worrying about him. I reminded him that we were coming up to visit the following Sunday and he was delighted. For once he had enjoyed a marvellous day out and quite obviously loved the fact that he had managed to cause a stir. This conversation with my father was different because he was so happy and that made it special. It was also the last conversation I was ever to have with him.

The next day he was knocked down and killed whilst trying to cross the road outside his home.

I was always close to my adopted father. I do not know if it was a daughter-father thing but although he did not create me he was my father. As such he gave me unconditional love and never questioned my actions. He knew that I was searching for my natural parents and indeed paid my airfare to New Zealand. He never commented on my search and seemed to take a positive interest in my discoveries. He was an immensely private man about large issues and yet could bellow about tiny problems. To many he was seen as a difficult and somewhat stubborn individual and it is true that he loved to battle with politicians and bureaucracy in general. Yet this man, born German and of Jewish descent, survived Dachau and the Holocaust, coming to England with nothing. He started again, leaving behind his homeland

and his family and creating a new future. He made himself British, not only by nationalisation but also by re-creating himself. After serving as a Captain in the British Army, he settled in London and began a difficult climb to the top of a sales profession. Apart from a slight German accent that always remained with certain letters of the alphabet he was, by all accounts, very British. Morality, integrity, a stiff upper lip, an instant love of the underdog and a slightly quirky character, all helped to make him my adorable father.

The shock and sudden flurry of actions that had to be carried out following dad's death jolted Ben out of his depression and into the role of primary carer for both my mother and me. He was wonderful and totally supportive.

The fact dad was elderly and had lived a full life, did not alter the shock of his death and the manner in which he died. It only reminded me of how short life is and how fragile we are as human beings. My dad had always seemed to me to be indestructible, a pillar of strength. I had never envisaged him dying this way.

Death brings with it many messages. Mortality and the reality that life is not only short but also can end at any moment; it also brings the stark truth that life goes on. As when my sister died I had the same feelings of unreality as I watched people going about their daily business. It was as though time itself had stopped for me and yet the world carried on. The result was a re-prioritising of my own personal values, hopes and ambitions. It is true that mundane daily tasks seem even more pointless when placed beside the enormity of a loss of a loved one. It is also true that death brings a renewal of bonds between family member by reinforcing the value and importance of individuals within a family.

The effect of my father's death on Ben gave him the ability to conquer the part of him that did not believe in himself and find a new strength to fight against the illness that had been caused by his overworking. Within a few months he had successfully won a battle with the company that caused the stress and more importantly, for his own sense of value, had been headhunted by a leading Defence Publisher.

Much as we, as a family were delighted in Ben's recovery the result was that in order for Ben to get to and from his new work on a daily basis, we would have to move house and area again.

My father's death made me realise how life can be erased in just a second or two. I felt a deep sense of anger at my time wasting, not only in my daily life but also at in the years spent struggling to find my natural relatives. All those years that were, forever lost. It highlighted for me importance of giving adopted adults full rights and total disclosure about natural adult family members. Many adoptees who wait, for whatever reason, until they are middle-aged before searching; find that once they have made this difficult decision to go ahead, they then begin the lengthy process of hacking their way through a jungle of red tape before obtaining any disclosing information. It made me wonder how many of these individuals then go on to discover that the person they are looking for has died and if the search had been made easier or information was centralised and fully available, they may have had a chance to be reunited.

I had a great sense of urgency to finish this search and to tie up all the loose ends. Because we were once again moving I was also very conscious that just twenty minutes down the road from us lived Louise's eldest son, Don and I felt that if I could just speak with him, just once, I might be able to finally piece everything together. I decided not to waste any more time waiting for Louise to speak with him and make contact with him directly

In my last conversation with Mary, she had spoken quite openly about Louise and the children. She had told me that Don had known about my birth. On the night she was discharged from hospital with me, she had nowhere to stay. Roland paid for her to stay in a pub, *The Dog and Fox* in Wimbledon. Roland had brought Don with him that night and ordered him to go a buy a cot for me. Don had returned with a cot and then they had left Mary at the pub.

I felt this man would remember, that he might have wondered for years what had happened that evening. I knew that this son was only fifteen years old at the time of my birth and I thought it likely that this boy probably knew all about his father's affair with Mary.

It was amazing to think that my first night outside hospital was spent in that particular pub in Wimbledon village, as this was the pub where Ben and I held our wedding reception. I found this a strangely comforting coincidence.

Throughout this search there have been some odd coincidences. Just before any reunion or contact has been made with a birth relative, a family member or close friend has died. The day my letter arrived at Mary's house, her beloved uncle died. Just before being reunited with John, a very close friend of mine died of Aids. Before being reunited with Roland, my sister Amy died and before being reunited with Karen, Lucinda our natural grandmother died. Coincidence or not it has lead me to have a great belief in viewing death as a new beginning. One door closing and another opening. Of course it may be the case that as a result of each death I have put renewed effort into searching again, but there has been an unexplained pattern of deaths and reunions.

With my father's death I really could not see that any reunion would match the loss I was experiencing. I had now found all close family members and was only trying to make some form of closure in a search that had dominated my life for so long. Contacting my half-brother was, I felt, more of a formality, and I could see no way that he would really want to know me. I knew that I would probably not want to know him if the tables were turned so I telephoned him whilst in a particularly non-caring mood.

A woman answered and I simply asked to speak with Mr G. She did not question me and handed the phone over to Don. On hearing his voice, I was immediately taken back; it was identical to his fathers, quiet with a soft Lancashire accent. I explained quickly who I was and that I believed "his father was my father."

Don did not sound shocked by my statement and in fact said he had been expecting my call. I thought this meant that Louise had already spoken to him about me but she had not. Don was so calm it was quite off-putting and left me shocked. Either he knew far more than he was saying, or, he was simply devoid of emotion. I was not quite sure how to react. I was used to people giving a surprised response but he seemed to be quite matter of fact about it all.

I asked if he would be interested in meeting and he quite calmly said that he would talk with his wife, Jane about it and get back to me some time.

Some time! I was stunned. The call finished and I made my way through the house to share this incredible conversation with Ben. He was also somewhat perplexed. Then the telephone rang. It was Don phoning back to apologise for being so calm! This made me laugh; it was as though he had been listening to me telling Ben about the conversation. Don said that he and his wife would like to me with us and we could either meet up at a pub or go over to his house. After a few more telephone calls between us that evening we decided to go over to his house the following week.

CHAPTER TWELVE

BOUNDARIES

Having so many other things going on in my life at this time I had given hardly any thought to this forthcoming reunion. It was only whilst on the way to Don and Jane's house that I began to feel quite anxious. This was due partly to the fact we were going to arrive late, having managed to get completely lost round the one way system through Basingstoke; and partly because for the first time I was about to meet a man who belonged to, and grew up within the natural family. Don would know all there was to know about his parents and their marriage, he would also know Mary.

Although I was delighted that he seemed keen to meet, I wondered why? I tried to imagine someone contacting me and saying that they were my father's child and would I like to meet. I found the thought disturbing. Again I had also not given any thought to Don's possible expectations and wondered whether his interest was perhaps in order to have an opportunity to express his anger at my having contacted his mother.

From what Mary had said it appeared that Louise had a hard time bring up her five children. Don being the eldest would have probably felt the most hardship and may have deep resentments about Mary. I was beginning to feel as I had done whilst talking to Louise, that I was treading on private ground. I was over-stepping acceptable family boundaries and perhaps being an unwanted trespasser.

I had during my telephone call backed out of telling Don that there were four of us. I had the feeling that Louise must have talked with him but when he had said that she had not mentioned me, I found that I just could not tell him. I knew that it would be kinder to tell him face to face, or not at all, depending on how friendly he was and how we got on.

As Ben parked the car we could see a woman, with short dark stylish hair and a huge excited smile, standing at the door of a large detached house. It was Jane and as we climbed out of the car she came towards us.

"God you can see the likeness," she said as I walked towards her. "Oh you *are* like Don." We kissed and were welcomed warmly into their home. Just inside the door stood Don, he was also smiling.

"Isn't she like you!" Jane continued. It is strange, as this time I was not expecting to look anything like Don. Before, when meeting one of my full-blood siblings I have been initially a little disappointed when there had not been a strong physical resemblance. Yet this time I could see the likeness quite clearly and I found it odd.

Don, like John and Martin, is tall, very tall, standing at six foot six inches. This is undoubtedly a similarity through the male line. Karen and Mary are above average height and so at five foot six inches, I am relatively short. Karen and Mary have identical colouring, both with rich dark hair and deep blue eyes. John and Martin both have brown hair and again blue eyes, but this time pale blue. I have fair-mousy hair and green eyes. Although I could not see direct likeness at the time of meeting my siblings, mannerisms and habits were in many ways far more revealing. How the genes are mixed and handed on have resulted in some uncanny similarities in mannerisms, habits and even deportment, rather than obvious similar physical features.

This time, however, I could not deny that there was a strong physical resemblance between Don and myself. Not only in facial features but also in skin tone and hair colouring.

For the first half-hour we all sat, slightly nervously, talking around the subject of family and making polite conversation. I noticed that Don was observing me just as I was him and found this quietly amusing. Jane was keeping the conversation going and in her no nonsense, Yorkshire manner making us feel quite relaxed. I had the strange feeling that I knew Don. Something in his manner and his personality was so familiar and yet I had not met him before. What I was recognising was someone incredibly similar to me. Even more so than Mary, this time I had an instant knowledge of how this person thought and what he was like.

On the discovery that we were all sinners and smoked, the tobacco appeared and within minutes we were all chatting as though we were old friends. I noticed that Don allowed Jane to do more of the talking as he observed, then when I felt quite at ease and the time seemed appropriate I asked if they had ever suspected that there might be more than one illegitimate child?

"What makes you say that?" Jane's answer was so quick that it took me by surprise. Her response immediately told me that they suspected or knew that there were more children around. I wanted her to tell me what she knew but she had quite firmly placed the question back at me and I knew she also wanted to know how much I understood of Roland's affairs.

I explained as I had done before that I was not the only "accident" born to Roland and Mary, that in fact there were others. Jane immediately began telling us how after Roland died, Louise had confided in them saying that she had been contacted by a woman who claimed to be trying to find Roland because he was the father of a young man who was searching for him. I realised that the woman Louise was talking about was me and that was the phone call I had with her back in 1989. Jane went on to say that Louise had not told them about the call until after Roland's death in 1995 and that Louise believed the young man was in the police force. Jane and Don had tried to find him through a police contact but had had no luck.

I told them that I was the woman who had contacted Louise and that the young man was John. I then told them about Karen and Martin. Don did not say anything. He did not appear shocked or surprised or at all angry at the information I was giving.

I then asked him what his father did for a living and he replied that his father was a journalist.

I went on to explain that Mary had told me that Roland had lived a double life. On one hand he was a journalist, married with five children and on the other he was a spy, working for various government departments and using Mary, not only as his mistress, but also as his informant.

Again Don did not appear shocked and did not deny Mary's stories; instead he just said that he was amazed, as I seemed to know more about his father than he did!

I did not understand but had the feeling that I had again stepped over a private boundary. I did not want to know more than he did, quite the reverse in fact as I really wanted to know whether it was all true and what, exactly had happened. Don then explained how his childhood had been anything but secure. How, as the eldest he was often sent to stay with other relatives as his parents struggle to cope.

It appeared that his childhood had been spent in several houses and places as Roland and Louise moved frequently to avoid the debt-collectors. It was a poor childhood, emotionally and physically and by the time Don was twelve he was regularly left to look after his four younger siblings.

Added to the real poverty he experienced were the frequent rows between his parents and wild parties that they held. Don did remember Mary, he also remembered being with his father when they picked her up and then having to sit quietly in a car whilst Roland and Mary held hands. Don knew that his father was having an affair with Mary but he did not ask or say anything. In those days children kept quiet and he would never have dreamed of questioning his father's actions.

The picture he painted of his family life was stark and desperate. He had grown up within his natural family, he had several brothers and a sister and yet because of his father's lifestyle, work and affairs he had not been given a chance to get close to his own siblings and had not really had a chance to be a boy. The consequences of his father's relationships and lifestyle had directly affected Don and all of his siblings.

The reality was that Don did not know his siblings well. There had been small moments in his childhood when he had experienced closeness with one of his siblings but even now, some fifty years later he did not have the bonds with his own family that I had with my adopted one. It seemed so sad that as a result of Mary and Roland's affair, there were so many lost siblings.

Throughout my search I held on to a belief that families who grew up together, even if they are separated by distance, have a natural bond, that binds them as a family unit. What Don was saying was a direct challenge to this. Although he obviously cared about his family members, it seemed that he and his siblings were just as much strangers to each other as we were. The history shared between Don and his family was disjointed and marked mainly by traumatic events, rather than the "magical" family memories made throughout Ben's childhood.

The saying "The grass is always greener," sprung into mind as I listened to Don talking. As an adoptee I had, whilst growing up always felt, like many other adopted people, that if I had grown up with my natural family I would have had parents who really understood me. Any family row, usually with my adopted mother brought out this feeling within me. My academic differences and personality clashes I blamed directly on being adopted. I lived in a fantasy that all the misunderstandings and unhappiness were simply because I was like a "cuckoo" in a robins nest.

What is often forgotten is that a child is placed for adoption because the natural family is truly unable to care for that child or because the natural family is so dysfunctional adoption is seen as the best option. Certainly having met Mary's family and indeed, Mary, and now listening to Don's account of his childhood where his own needs were almost completely ignored; the reality was that Mary had, without thought, and certainly without consciousness, actually done the best thing possible in giving us all up.

My upbringing, compared to Don's, had been remarkably privileged. I had never gone hungry or cold or moved from place to place to avoid trouble. Although there was no closeness between my mother and me and my father was often away, I did not want for any material things. Our home life was secure with my parents totally in control of their lives and our welfare.

As the evening progressed I found myself puzzled by how well we got on. Our upbringings could not have been more different. Our experiences in life, work and home, "poles apart" yet this man was more similar to me in personality, character and sense of humour than any other natural relative. What was also wonderful was that as a foursome we all formed a friendship.

Perhaps, through our differences in life's experiences we have both always wanted the same thing. A sense of belonging, of a closeness within a family. Over the last decade John and I have shared experiences and now have made a history together which enforces our relationship as brother and sister.

It was a sad thought that combining Roland and Louise's children and Roland and Mary's children there were nine siblings all who had been brought up differently and yet all who might be wanting a sense of belonging. I was reminded of the title of a play by Pirandello, *Six Characters in Search of an Author*, and thought of us in a similar way.

When I was a child my thoughts about finding my natural parents focused mainly on my mother. I was constantly looking at women, of a mother's age, trying to find something about that person with which I could identify. I seldom thought about my natural father. If I did it was always a formal setting. I would have found him and unknown to him, made an appointment to see him. I would wait outside his office, and then when called in have some completely plausible reason for being there. I never looked at men in the street for a likeness as I had a clear picture in my head of what he would be like.

His office would be large, leather chairs and a huge desk. He would be concentrating on his work and I would wait politely until he looked up. I saw him as a tall distinguished middle-aged man with fair, silver hair and a rugged, but gentle face.

This fantasy was of course created from mixing my respect and love for my adopted father and his distinguished features with my own colouring. I found it revealing that Don fitted not only the physical image of my imaginary natural father but being a Director of a large mobile telephone firm, also spent his days at the office. I also found it a little spooky that Don and Jane lived and worked in Basingstoke, as this is where my father spent most of his working life.

What had begun as just a formality was becoming a wonderful reunion with a relative that I really had no reason to meet. Yet through meeting Don I have, at last found the "set" to which I belong. It is extraordinarily comforting to find someone who is like you. The true nature of the relationship between my natural parents will never be answered fully, as they were, so secretive and possessive that it was a particularly selfish affair that did not take into account the consequences of their actions.

The children born firstly within the marriage and then the ones within the affair really did not matter at all. Those children, however, all grown and spanning in age from early thirties to mid fifties, all have different stories to tell of their own life experiences.

Don and I spent much time talking about siblings and their lack of rights to have information about one another when parted through adoption. It is an area that is poorly served partly because the majority of adopted people are single accidents and partly because the needs of adopted people normally focused on the birth or natural parents and the assumption that an adoptee is only interested in their parentage.

There were undoubtedly things that Don knew about his father that he was either not prepared to talk about or had placed at the back of his mind. Just by watching and listening to what he said and what he avoided saying, I found I was understanding the unspoken language between us. Like me, Don is interested in people, how they think and what they are all about. This curiosity in individuals has groomed us both to be always polite and careful with our actions when in company.

I was amazed by how stable he was. Always calm, always appearing to be at ease with life. I wondered if this was a direct result of his lost childhood and his parents' erratic relationship and lifestyle.

Not many people could survive the hardships he experienced without carrying some "baggage". The only slightly quirky behaviour trait discovered was a tendency to check plugs and "water" cigarette ends. This was something I knew very well as, in the past I had driven not only Ben, but several of my friends to screaming at me because of my inability to leave a house without going back for just one last check!

As Jane told me about Don's one maddening habit I realised that I now held the proof that conditioning through upbringing and environment cannot alter an individual's genetic predisposition to certain behaviour or inherited traits. The proof existed with us, as siblings separated at birth and having had entirely different upbringings within different social and economic surroundings; some of us shared the most absurd similarities. Don, John and I all bite our nails, down to the core. Don and John both have a habit of sitting with one leg crossed at a right-angle over the other and then, dare I say it removing their socks and smelling them, rolling them into a ball and chucking them aside to enjoy a good pick at the toenails. It is not the revolting habit but the way in which this ritual is performed is identical. As with this absurd habit, body language, use of hands when taking, sense of humour and facial expressions used are all similar between us.

Karen, as I have said before, walks identically to Mary. Not just in the way she carries herself, but also the way she uses her hand gestures when speaking. Her voice, her laugh and her expressions are identical and yet they have never met.

Don, Karen and I all share an interest in writing. We all have that "bug" that enjoys being creative on paper. Don is also a gifted artist. John and I play the piano and it is almost too uncanny how identical some of the tunes are. Don and I both swam competitively, both at county and national level, both racing the same stroke. John boxed and reached national level as Roland had done before him.

If you grow up within your natural family, the similarities between you seem natural and the physical likeness is taken for granted, whereas the behavioural likeness quite often seen as the nurturing bit. What I have found most extraordinary in this search is the reverse is far truer.

Over the next few months we got together with Don and Jane several times and each time we have discovered more similarities between us. As when I first met John I wish it was possible to catch up quickly on making a history together but as adults with our own lives it is a slower process that is dictated to by our busy and varying lives.

When I watch my children playing or fighting together, I realise what has been lost. Brothers and sisters who grow up together may not get along with each other but if they stop for one moment to think about their sibling, they have an instant feeling and understanding of that child in their mind. This is not something that siblings can achieve when separated until adulthood.

What has been lost however is not relevant when I realise what I have found in searching for my natural relatives. This search has brought together many souls who have made the choice of whether or not to continue meeting. Who says you can't pick your family, in many respects that is exactly what we have all done. One advantage is that although I am linked to each person I have found, I do not have any obligations towards them and they also, have no obligations towards me. In that respect reunited adopted adults are people who freely create their own extended family and a unique history between them.

I have often thought how lucky I am to be someone who is able to buy two "Mother's Day" cards. One for the lady who made me and one for the lady who brought me up. If you take a moment to look at cards for mothers, sisters, brothers and children, it is often quite difficult to find a card that appropriately expresses the feelings felt for natural relatives. Again the cards have boundaries of their own within the flowery words and sentiments. I have often wondered how long it will be before a card appears for "My egg donating mother".

CHAPTER THIRTEEN

FULL CIRCLE

It is late November 2002 and I have just returned from visiting my mother, the lady who brought me up. To all the staff who work in the residential home where she now lives, we are seen as a mother and daughter who are exceptionally close. It has, in fact taken some forty years to find an "understanding" with my mother and now as I look back I feel blessed to have been given the opportunity, however late, to experience a wonderful and loving relationship with her.

It seems bizarre that the dreadful breakdown in our relationship that dominated my childhood and probably initiated my desire to search has finally become the relationship that I so longed for as a child.

In 1961 when I came to my parents, my mother was a different person. Already in her late forties she lived within a world where people did not openly discuss personal issues. You kept a "stiff upper lip" and always appeared to your friends and neighbours as untroubled, upright and a part of a solid family unit. Preferably middle-class, undoubtedly married with just the right amount of children (one of each sex), she was a busy housewife, involving herself in activities that fitted her social status. Intelligent and quite capable of being a top businesswoman, my mother kept herself very busy. With a cleaner and an au pair to help her in the home, she was able to immerse herself in her studies and that gave her the opportunity to form friendships with other educated women of the same class.

It is hard to image a time when the class system basically classified what type of person you were and which people were suitable to associate with. Although my mother had an enormously interesting and varied life, she never disclosed to her friends that she had a severely handicapped daughter or that my brother and I were adopted. Those personal pieces of information were simply not discussed.

I think that for most of my childhood my mother must have been suffering from depression due to the never-ending grief she suffered at having to part with her own daughter. To give up your own child to another couple is traumatic enough but to give up your own child into the cold environment of institutional life is, thankfully now unimaginable. Counselling as a serious option did not exist; you were far more likely to be told by your doctor to "pull yourself together" or offered psychiatric help and for my mother, only the first option would have been socially acceptable. Therefore the only way of dealing with a personal tragedy was to never discuss it. I am in no doubt that if my mother had been encouraged to express her sadness and if the openness that we have with our children today, had existed; the misunderstandings between us would have been far less damaging.

It has taken forty years for us both to realise that we were both, in fact, searching. Mum was searching for the daughter she had lost and I was searching for a mother figure who would understand me. It may not be the most perfect timing, but now, when she is very frail, severely arthritic and in her eighty-seventh year and I am at the beginning of my fourth decade, with children of my own, we have finally managed to become a devoted mother and daughter.

As with the years that I have lost with my natural relatives, my mother and I lost many years through the misunderstandings over the different expectations we had about each other and this was made worse by our simple lack of communication. One of the hardest things I had to justify when beginning this search was doing something that would directly cause my adopted mother pain. Although our relationship was not close, I did not want to make matters worse between us and in fact would have done anything to gain her praise. I knew that embarking on this quest would only create more of a wedge between us. The problem was very simply that I was looking for a person with the same title as her.

The title "mother" or "father" presents many problems for an adopted people because these two labels are of such fundamental importance to all children and they are quite often, and rightly so, viewed with reverence. Often this is the reason why adoptees do not begin their search until both their adopted parents are dead.

A mother is someone who gives life, through birth and nurtures her offspring until maturity. When two women share this process as in a birth mother, bringing forth a life and an adopted mother rearing that child, they then share the same "honoured" title. So it is easy to see how this brings about a huge problem, not only for the two mothers involved but also for the adopted child who wishes to find the "other mother."

Similarly a child considers the title "father" with utmost respect for a man who is regarded as a stable, authoritative figurehead of the family and who, through his strength but gentleness guides and protects his own family. An adopted father may, be deeply wounded that his position and purpose within the family unit is threatened. An adoptee cannot prevent all upsets within the home by disclosing that he or she wishes to search but nor should the adopted person be so wrapped in guilt at the thought of searching that they delay it until it is too late.

As an adoptee the guilt I felt at starting this search was caused mainly because of these titles. I wanted to find my birth/natural/real/biological mother. It did not matter which variation was used, in my adopted mother's eyes I could only see her connecting with the word "mother". Try as I did to never refer to the woman who gave birth to me as "mother" I was most relieved once I knew her name. To be able to talk with my parents about finding Mary and not have to use the words birth mother made the search much less stressful for both my parents and myself.

I could have decided as many adoptees do, not to tell my adopted parents that I was searching. In many ways this would have been a much easier route to take but I am a firm believer that sensitive secrets, if kept too long, have a nasty way of backfiring on you.

During the last twenty-five years I have met many adopted people and been quite surprised to find that so many of them take this risk.

One friend of mine also adopted chose this route believing that it was the kindest way to protect her adopted parents. Some years later when she had successfully formed a relationship with her natural mother, she was staying with her children at her adopted parent's home. It was Mothering Sunday and the whole family had gone to church. During the service the children were asked to go up to the front and collect a bunch of daffodils for their mothers and grandmothers. On returning to their pews, one of her children had collected three bunches of daffodils. She gave one to her mother and one to her grandmother and then placed the remaining bunch on her lap. Her grandmother bent forward to ask the little girl why she had taken three bunches and the child answered that she was keeping them for "my other grandma, mummy's secret mother."

Unless an adoptee can be absolutely certain that their adopted parents will not find out third-hand (which is often more hurtful again), I do feel it is best to be open about searching from the beginning. Although both my parents knew, I never talked with them about individual searches or the progress I was making, I waited for them to ask me. My mother never asked about Mary or Roland but quite often they would ask me questions about my siblings.

My adopted mother was hurt when I first told her of my wish to search. She did not understand and this was because it looked as though by searching for a replacement mother. Many years later she confided in me and said that if she had been adopted she would have wanted to know about her past. I was so happy that she told me this as it lifted the years of feeling guilty away and reassured me that, in part, she recognised my need. Undoubtedly the length of time this search has taken also helped as, time itself has diffused the impact on my parents and also shown that throughout subsequent years we have still remained just the same. Again the fact that Mary lives in New Zealand and my birth father is dead, certainly provided a reassurance to my parents, that I could not simply "pop" round for coffee with either one of my birth parents and so the initial worries that my search brought, have gone.

I have always felt that a mother is the one who does the bringing up of a child. Mary is the lady who brought me into this world, giving me life and providing me with my genetic inheritance. Having met and now formed a friendship with her I have been able to recognise quite a few personality traits that has proved most beneficial to understanding more about myself. It also allows me to understand what medical problems, both physically and emotionally, my children might face in the future and maybe I can be more equipped to deal with them.

I find a strange irony in the heated debates our government had surrounding the last White Paper on adoption and the possibility of single women and gay couples being allowed to adopt. In just a few decades the very women who were forced to give up their babies, are now being considered as respectable adopters.

Recently I was talking with my twelve-year old son about adoption and trying to explain why I had been given up. I explained how Mary had been a single woman.

So?" He replied, "What's that got to do with it?"

His answer said it all. Today's society and the way we think, judge and label people has changed beyond all expectations. Single mothers are no longer discriminated against; the women who gave up their babies purely because they were not married are viewed with sympathy.

The imperfect child is no longer hidden away but encouraged to receive an education and to achieve as much independence as possible within a community. The huge impersonal Institutions have either been knocked down or, as I have noticed, become historic features within new housing estates.

As a more tolerant society takes shape and scientific advances allow for babies to be conceived outside the womb, so adoption has also changed. Closed adoption where all links with the past were severed, is no longer the normal path. Instead, there are now various levels of contact made with a child's natural parents. Either information and letters from the natural parents are kept in the child's adoption file until he or she is eighteen; or yearly up-dates, through video are sent both from the adopted child to the natural parents and vice-versa. The openness brought in has provided the adopted child with another precious piece of information and that is a detailed family medical history, one denied to anyone involved in a "closed" adoption before 1975.

Many a time I have been given some medical form to fill out, only to find myself writing "adopted" across it. Yet by searching for my family history I have discovered that, for instance, diabetes runs through the male side of the family. Having two sons of my own I have now been able to place this important information on their medical records. Cancer also makes frequent appearances on both sides of my natural family. With the advance in genetic testing for certain diseases and Insurance companies waiting to pounce on us for our most medically revealing information, I do, happily, still retain the right to scrawl "adopted" across any type of form and then wait to see which category I am placed in. For those people involved in closed adoption who have never searched, their medical history will be unknown to them and to their children and so for this alone, I find the openness of information now available to adoptees, most sensible.

It should be noted however that the changes that have taken place in Adoption Law and the rights of adopted adults to obtain their original birth certificates have never been extended to include birth mothers and fathers. As a country we still lag behind many other nations by not giving, equality to these men and women, many of whom are now aged sixty and older. Many birth parents do not wish to "invade" their child's life but spend their lives wondering what became of that child and whether or not he or she is still alive? A register of adopted people's deaths may provide a non-contact way of providing many birth parents with this answer. It would not be difficult for a birth parent simply to apply to the Registrar General for this information. The Registrar General is the only person who is able to cross-match an original birth entry with the identity of an adopted person. A register could quite easily be compiled which would, at least, provide a well-needed answer for many, now elderly birth parents.

I once sat next to a birth mother at a wedding. I was not aware that she was the bridegroom's birth mother but she had been told that I would "understand" her situation. I shared four very emotional hours in her company as she watched her son get married and then after being introduced to the family as "a friend", she sat with me at the reception and shared the occasion as a guest. Her son had wanted her there for his special day and yet he did not want his adopted parents to feel awkward or upset. It was a very moving occasion and one that highlights, for me, the position of anyone involved in the adoption triangle. It is the role of being the outsider, looking in. You are involved with all the people that make up your adopted family and your natural family and yet, in a way you do not ever fully belong to either.

Some advances in the world of adoption do remain questionable and curious to me. With the priority now placed firmly with the child who is being given up for adoption, the "suitability" tests that prospective adopters had to go through in the past have now become almost an intrusion into every part of their personal and private lives. With the numbers of babies available for adoption decreased due to the acceptance of single mothers, the pill, abortion and sex education, the number of people wanting babies far out weighs the numbers of babies available. There are of course always older children needing homes and these are still, often bypassed for the chance of having a new-born.

Infertile couples have many choices now. IVF has cleared the way for a variety of options. Surrogate motherhood, sperm donating fathers and now egg donating mothers, have resulted in so many alternatives to the simple idea of adoption. In our Brave New World it really does seem viable that one day in the future it will be possible to "grow your own" baby outside the womb.

When I think of the modern techniques used in the treatment of infertile couples I begin to wonder whether the children born as a result of donor sperm or eggs will grow up to fight for the right to search for their biological parents. It conjures up various scenarios about the possibilities of fifty or even one hundred people turning up on one donor's doorstep declaring that he or she is their birth parent. I wonder if the donated eggs are given to people in different areas of the country or whether a whole batch of eggs is successfully placed within women who live in one small area? What are the chances of these children growing up and innocently forming relationships with each other, unaware of their genetic bond? Are there measures being taken to prevent this or is there a real danger of in-breeding facing those future adults? At present, any parent of a baby born through egg or sperm donation has the right to medical information about the donor that might be beneficial to the child. Who can say, however, when these children grow up that they will not want to know more about their literally "biological" parent. It is, I think, going to result in some very unusual scenarios and reunions in the future.

I am still in contact with Mary. We write and telephone regularly, but the sheer distance between us does not help to reinforce the bonds. I am aware that my brothers, sister and I all exist because of hundreds of secret sexual moments, snatched between our birth parents, whilst on trains, commons and cars. We were not as I always thought "love-babies" but "lust-babies" produced in a relationship that had no room for anyone else other than the leading players. I accept Mary the way she is, for me it is more important that I now try to be the mother that I always wanted, for my own children. In that respect I have found what I was looking for through my relationship with my own children.

I am completely glad that I made this journey. It has brought many new people into my life and with them some wonderful new friendships. It has not been an easy search; most of it was carried out before there were advisory services and organisations available to help, or to lend a sympathetic "ear". I have been blessed by being given a husband who is remarkably patient and who has had to live through the not so wonderful parts of this search with me. I am now ready to move on into a new and hopefully enjoyable phase of life and that is to "make some history" with my natural relatives, especially my siblings.

Most of the reunions have gone through what is called a "honeymoon" period, where the sheer excitement of making contact with a natural relative has brought with it a huge sense of instant fulfilment. It is only now that this initial phase has passed that the real "getting to know someone" begins. In a sense it will always a beginning because with the pasts missing between us all there are always new things to learn and discover about each other.

I have gained lots of new family and my children are slowly getting used to having an ever-growing selection of new aunts, uncles and cousins. Our Christmas and birthday budget has gone through the roof, but really it is a small price to pay for a rich journey that has brought me, full circle, back home to my own family, past, present and future.

Being adopted has taken me down a long path of discovery that has forced me to think deeply about how I value relationships within both my adopted and natural families. It has also made me immensely curious about people, whether it is the way a person looks, speaks, moves or behaves. I find I am always drawn to noticing similarities between individuals. I no longer follow strangers home, the missing faces and identities are now all known to me, but I will never stop being addicted to people. It's only natural!

USEFUL ADDRESSES

The following organisations offer confidential advice and counselling services.

NORCAP
112 Church Road
Wheatley
Oxfordshire
OX33 1LU
Tel: 01865 875000

NORCAP not only gives advice but has a contact register. They provide a wide range of services. It's worth checking out their web site www. NORCAP.org

THE POST ADOPTION CENTRE
5 Torriano Mews
Kentish Town
London NW5 2RZ
Tel: 0207 2840555

NATURAL PARENTS' NETWORK
C/O Sheila Walker
79 Crockford Park Road
Addlestone
Surrey KT15 2LN Tel: 01932 838930

BIRTHLINK
Family Care
21 Castle Street
Edinburgh EH2 3DN
Tel: 0131 225 6441

NATIONAL CONTACT REGISTER

If you place your details on this register and the person you are seeking also does the same then you will be matched. Siblings remember to place your details on both parts of the application form. There is a fee for this service

OFFICE OF NATIONAL STATISTICS
The General Register Office
Adoptions Section
Smedley Hydro
Trafalgar Road
Southport PR8 2HH

All records of Births, Marriages and Deaths are housed at the Public Records Office. Records are no longer kept at St. Catherine's House.

PUBLIC RECORDS OFFICE
Chancery Lane
London WC2A 1LP